Grupo Prisa

In one of the first English-language studies of Grupo Prisa, this book delivers a comprehensive and concise approach to the political, economic, and social-cultural profile of one of the leading cross-media conglomerates in Europe, tracing its development from a single newspaper publisher in 1972.

Prisa is now the world's leading Spanish- and Portuguese-language media group in the creation and distribution of content in the fields of culture, education, and information, producing content for more than 20 countries with global brands like *El País* (newspaper), Los 40 (radio), and Santillana (education). Using a critical political economy approach, the authors track Prisa's journey to becoming a cross-media conglomerate and examine how it mirrors the recent history of the economic and political developments in Spain.

This concise and highly contemporary volume is ideal for students, scholars, and researchers looking to further their understanding of a growing Spanish-language media power or more generally interested in international communication and media industries.

Luis A. Albornoz is Associate Professor in the Department of Communication Studies at Carlos III University of Madrid (UC3M), and director of the research group Audiovisual Diversity (www.diversidadaudiovisual.org). He is director of the MA in Applied Research to Mass Media at UC3M. He is also founding partner and former president (2007–2013) of the international scientific association Latin Union of Political Economy of Information, Communication and Culture (ULEPICC).

Ana I. Segovia is Associate Professor in the Department of Journalism and New Media at Complutense University of Madrid (UCM). She is founding partner and president of the Spanish section of the international scientific association Latin Union of Political Economy of Information, Communication and Culture (ULEPICC). Her research interest includes communication policies and global media corporations.

Núria Almiron is Associate Professor in the Department of Communication at Pompeu Fabra University (UPF). She is director of the UPF research group Audiovisual Communication Research Unit (UNICA), coordinator of the THINKClima research project, and director of the UPF's MA in International Studies in Media, Power and Difference.

Global Media Giants
Series editors: Benjamin J. Birkinbine, Rodrigo Gomez and Janet Wasko

Since the second half of the 20th century, the significance of media corporate power has been increasing in different and complex ways around the world; the power of these companies in political, symbolic and economic terms has been a global issue and concern. In the 21st century, understanding media corporations is essential to understanding the political, economic and sociocultural dimensions of our contemporary societies.

The **Global Media Giants** series continues the work that began in the series editors' book *Global Media Giants*, providing detailed examinations of the largest and most powerful media corporations in the world.

For more information about this series, please visit: www.routledge.com/Global-Media-Giants/book-series/GMG

Alphabet
The Becoming of Google
Micky Lee

Tencent
The Political Economy of China's Surging Internet Giant
Min Tang

Grupo Prisa
Media Power in Contemporary Spain
Luis A. Albornoz, Ana I. Segovia and Núria Almiron

Grupo Prisa
Media Power in Contemporary Spain

Luis A. Albornoz, Ana I. Segovia
and Núria Almiron

NEW YORK AND LONDON

First published 2020
by Routledge
52 Vanderbilt Avenue, New York, NY 10017

and by Routledge
2 Park Square, Milton Park, Abingdon, Oxon, OX14 4RN

Routledge is an imprint of the Taylor & Francis Group, an informa business

© 2020 Taylor & Francis

The right of Luis A. Albornoz, Ana I. Segovia, and Núria Almiron to be identified as authors of this work has been asserted by them in accordance with sections 77 and 78 of the Copyright, Designs and Patents Act 1988.

All rights reserved. No part of this book may be reprinted or reproduced or utilised in any form or by any electronic, mechanical, or other means, now known or hereafter invented, including photocopying and recording, or in any information storage or retrieval system, without permission in writing from the publishers.

Trademark notice: Product or corporate names may be trademarks or registered trademarks, and are used only for identification and explanation without intent to infringe.

Library of Congress Cataloging-in-Publication Data
A catalog record for this book has been requested

ISBN: 978-0-367-27753-6 (hbk)
ISBN: 978-0-429-29771-7 (ebk)

Typeset in Times New Roman
by Apex CoVantage, LLC

Contents

	Acknowledgements	vi
1	Introduction	1
2	History	8
3	Economic Profile	26
4	Political Profile	47
5	Cultural Profile	71
6	Conclusion	102
	Index	110

Acknowledgements

The authors would like to thank the many colleagues who, over the years in our academic careers, have helped us build a consistent line of work on the case of Grupo Prisa, supported our research, and enriched it with their comments, especially the academic network created by the international scientific association Latin Union of Political Economy of Information, Communication and Culture (ULEPICC).

We also would like to thank the Routledge staff (many thanks, Emma, for your patience!) and, in particular, the series editors of Global Media Giants and our colleagues of the Political Economy Section of the International Association for Media and Communication Research–IAMCR (Ben, Rodrigo, and Janet) for their trust, encouragement, and support throughout the entire writing and editing processes of this volume.

Finally, we must thank those who are always the mainstays of any author: family members and friends. They are obliged to bear intense and prolonged periods of absence by the authors during weekends and holiday times. As always, we couldn't have made it without all of you. Thanks!!

# 1 Introduction

It is widely accepted that Spain is a country with a high degree of parallelism between media and politics. Political parallelism, as defined by Hallin and Mancini (2004), refers to the links between political actors and media actors, or, more precisely, the extent to which media reflects political divisions and struggles. In southern European countries, high political parallelism produces a media system that is extremely polarized – as political systems have been in the region – and instrumentalized. In Spain, this political polarization and instrumentalization of the media system meant for a long time that the mainstream media followed the bipartisan model of the political system, with outlets backing one of the two main political parties which alternated power and generated strong clientelistic ties (Fernández-Quijada and Arboledas, 2013). This changed in 2014, when new political parties emerged that embodied more radical positions on the left and the right than the two larger mainstream parties.

This new scenario transformed Spanish politics into a much more fragmented arena for the first time since the end of the Francoist regime in 1975, ending bipartisanship and bringing the political system closer to the diverse sociological reality of the country. However, the media system did not adapt to this reality since only the new right wing parties' views were incorporated into the mainstream media. By the end of 2017, for instance, the political views of citizens represented by 31.3 per cent of the members of the Spanish Parliament (who had voted for left wing Podemos or for pro-independence Catalan parties) were not reflected in the Spanish mainstream media. Therefore, political parallelism theory seems to collapse in Spain during this process.

The turbulence and dysfunction experienced by the Spanish media system since the recovery of democracy is the necessary beginning for any understanding of Grupo Prisa (Promotora de Informaciones S.A.), the media group to which this volume is devoted. A flagship brand of the democratic restoration in Spain, Prisa's birth, success, and decline meticulously reflects the Spanish media system's – and the whole country's – developments and struggles, including the communication policy and the liberalization of the broadcasting market. There is no way of deciphering Prisa's history if we omit the Spanish political peculiarities of the period or the political turmoil, such as the attempted coup d'état in 1981.

Hence, El País, Grupo Prisa's first and still most influential media asset, was the first pro-democracy newspaper within a context where all the other Spanish newspapers were influenced by Franco's ideology. However, the company founded to launch the newspaper was, and still is, far from being detached from the dictator's legacy. The newspaper, much like the whole group, was also born bearing the standard of journalistic independence and democratic responsibility. Yet, the fast and hazardous corporate growth the company has experienced is irresistibly linked to the particular version of financialization taking place in the Spanish economy, which has proven to be particularly harmful for journalistic independence and democratic values.

For this very reason, Grupo Prisa's history perfectly mirrors the specificities of the restored democracy in Spain, which, as in other southern European countries, has huge democratic deficits because of their recent authoritarian past. Prisa's corporate history, as with Spain's recent history, has plenty of ups and downs, including undemocratic taboos, political partisanship and clientelism, financial irrationality, power struggles, patriotism, and authoritarian neoliberalism.

The Neoliberal Storm and the Case of Spain

In the late twentieth century, the vested interests of media organizations and the corporate system were transformed by the financialization of capitalism, pushed forward by neoliberal proponents. As media corporations became absorbed by financial capitalism, their ownership structures concentrated further in an environment of greater instability and competitiveness. Consequently, news content became further distanced from its social responsibility criteria. The media's investigative and watchdog role was thereby radically diminished.

At the global level, media corporation links with the financial system made it difficult for journalists to denounce the 2007–2008 global financial crisis that began in the United States, and later spread to Europe and the rest of the world. At the Spanish level, Grupo Prisa is a unique example of this perfect storm that financialization produced by pushing financial interests into the media corporations, thus undermining the capacity of journalists to warn of the increasing weakness of an economic system based on finance rather than on real output.

Financialization, the increasing dominance of finance over the real economy, added to the problems of Western media systems – mostly commoditization and concentration – and its consequences are highly visible in the Spanish media system. Since the old fascist regime ended, most of the mainstream media in Spain have belonged to four big Spanish conglomerates: Grupo Prisa, Grupo Vocento, Grupo Planeta, and Telefónica. Two large Italian holding companies, Grupo Mediaset and RCS MediaGroup, were also involved in broadcasting and press, respectively. And two small Catalan groups, Grupo Godó and Grupo Zeta, published the two newspapers of record in Barcelona. All of them, without exception, hold strong ties with the corporate and financial elite. During the period of time we track in this volume for Prisa, all parent companies of the Spanish mainstream media were closely involved with the banking system through ownership, representation on boards of directors, and/or debt. Thus, several parent companies of the Spanish mainstream media (Prisa, Vocento, Mediaset, RCS) had stockholders from all of the top Spanish banking entities, international banks, and investment or hedge funds.

Grupo Prisa, for example, had a London hedge fund as the majority stockholder at least from 2016 to 2020. Some directors of the parent companies also served on the boards of other companies listed on the IBEX 35, the main stock market index of the Madrid Stock Exchange, during that period. Godó's chairman, for instance, was director of Caixa Bank, Planeta's chairman was director of Banco Sabadell, and Vocento's chairman was also director of the major Spanish construction company Ferrovial. Every parent company of Spanish mainstream media organizations had financial debts that compromised their business to a greater or lesser extent. In the case of Prisa, for instance, the impact of its debt brought about changes in its board of directors, who have been increasingly replacing independent directors with representatives of financial investors and creditors.

Of course, as mentioned, the links of the Spanish mainstream media with the financial and business elite are not their only feature. The origins of the Prisa, Vocento, Planeta, and Godó groups are clearly located in the old regime, with founders (or their descendants) maintaining control until the end of the second decade of the twenty-first century.

In the case of Prisa, the founding family still retained a very important stake in the company's ownership as of 2020 – even if its equity share went down to 7.6 per cent. It is worth remembering that the founder, Jesús Polanco, was a successful, Catholic, Falangist entrepreneur in the Franco's regime (Cabrera, 2015). He hired Juan Luis Cebrián as the editor in chief of *El País* at the end of the dictatorship (1975) because the latter had the "perfect pedigree" for the Francoist leaders attempting to direct the political transition (Seoane and Sueiro, 2004: 53).

4 Introduction

In Grupo Vocento, a conglomerate created after the merger of two centenary media groups (Grupo Correo and Prensa Española), it was still possible in 2020 to find the founding family within the ownership structure. The creator of *ABC* newspaper, Torcuato Luca de Tena, was a Catholic, pro-monarchy, Spanish patriot who combined his political stance with the editorial line of the newspaper. *ABC* was embedded into the so-called Prensa del Movimiento during Franco's dictatorship. The Prensa del Movimiento was the only legally allowed Spanish journalistic group during Franco's dictatorship and belonged to the regime's only party, the Falange Española de las JONS (Juntas de Ofensiva Nacional-Sindicalista). The founders of *ABC* were awarded aristocratic titles by King Alfonso XIII (1886–1941) in 1929 and King Juan Carlos I (1938–) in 2003, including the highest such title in Spain (Grande de España).

Grupo Planeta is still owned by the Lara family. Its founder, José Manuel Lara Hernández (1914–2003), also held an aristocratic title (Marqués de Pedroso), granted by the King of Spain, and participated in the Spanish Civil War on the Francoist side. At the end of the war, he entered Barcelona as captain of the Spanish legion and actively participated in the political repression in Catalonia. Lara Hernández became head of the Vertical Union of Graphic Arts, the only legal union, which was controlled by the Francoist regime during the dictatorship (EL PAÍS, 2003).

Grupo Godó is grounded in the century-old newspaper *La Vanguardia*, which was also embedded in the Prensa del Movimiento under Franco. The strong and public support of Javier Godó (1941–), the owner of the group, for the Spanish monarchy is well known. Like the founders of Vocento, he belongs to the Spanish aristocracy through two titles, Count and Grande de España, both awarded by the former King of Spain Juan Carlos I.

Telefónica is the biggest telecommunications company in Spain, with an outstanding presence in Latin America. The company was created in Madrid in 1924 as Compañía Telefónica Nacional de España (CTNE), with ITT as one of its major shareholders. It became mainly public in 1945 under Franco's dictatorship. The liberalization of the telecommunication market in the 1990s led to the complete privatization of the company. Telefónica operates pay-TV in Spain and Latin America through the brand Movistar+, and in Brazil through Vivo TV. As we will mention in Chapter 2, Telefónica's presence in the pay-TV market in Spain is profoundly linked to Prisa.

Mediaset Spa is an Italian media group active in the television sector, audio-visual production, and the Internet. In particular, it controls the first private television channels in Italy: Canale 5, Italia 1, and Rete 4. The group is associated with Silvio Berlusconi (1936–) and his family, the main shareholder through its holding company Fininvest (which also has a controlling interest in Mondadori, the most important publishing group in Italy).

Introduction 5

In Spain, Mediaset, whose trade name is Mediaset España Comunicación, is a media group created in March 1989. Its main activity is the production and exhibition of television content. It currently operates the free-to-air television channels Telecinco, Cuatro, Factoría de Ficción, Boing, Divinity, Energy, and Be Mad. It also owns several companies as part of its business group, including the news agency Atlas, the advertising manager Publiespaña, and the film and television audio-visual production company Telecinco Cinema. In 2019, Mediaset España and Mediaset Spa announced their merged into MFE NV (Media For Europe).

Rizzoli-Corriere della Sera MediaGroup (RCS MediaGroup) is an Italian holding company owner of daily newspapers and magazines, as well as radio and television broadcasting. It is also active in the sale and distribution of advertising. Its newspaper titles include *Corriere della Sera* (published since 1876) and *La Gazzetta dello Sport* in Italy. In Spain, RCS MediaGroup has the newspapers *El Mundo*, *Marca* (sports), and *Expansión* (business); magazines like *Yo Donna*, *Telva*, *Marca Motor*, *Actualidad Económica*, *Fuera de Serie*, and *Diario Médico*; the radio network Radio Marca (sports); and the licence of two free-to-air television channels (Veo TV).

All of this is relevant to understanding the values which complement financial capitalism and neoliberalism within the Spanish media system. The links with financial capitalism cannot by themselves explain the shortcomings of the Spanish mainstream media during the period; the political legacy of the old regime must be also taken into account. The same links are found everywhere in financialized capitalist democracies. However, the Spanish mainstream media groups' historic links with the old regime are a peculiarity of the Spanish media system.

Spanish capitalism is dominated by a narrow circle of descendants from the former Francoist oligarchy. Across the media system, financial debt prevented the media groups that have emerged after the democratic transition from escaping this pattern.

Grupo Prisa and Plan for the Book

Prisa's corporate behaviour and unfolding since its birth in 1972 until 2020 is probably among the most revealing examples of how neoliberalism and financialization promote and increase the weakening of social and corporate responsibility – and thus the weakening of democratic values.

In spite of having a larger number of shareholders at its birth and a hedge fund in control of the major portion of its ownership at the end of the studied period in this volume, the group was under the control of two men alone for its initial four decades of life: first under Jesús Polanco's hand, who managed to become the major stockholder until his death in 2007, and until 2018, under Juan Luis Cebrián's ruling, who raised the banking debt of the group to an impossible pay back (more than five billion euros at the highest point) and still managed to quit the company with a multimillionaire compensation. This was not an exception. For the majority of Western media moguls, making their companies public didn't mean losing direct control. Nevertheless, looking for capital resources in the capital markets brought them enormous pressure in terms of financial results. This meant a radical weakening of journalistic responsibility in general, which in the case of grupo Prisa added to the deficit of Spanish democracy (Almiron, 2010, 2018).

This book, whose direct antecedent is the publication of the chapter "Grupo Prisa" by Luis A. Albornoz (2016) in the book *Global Media Giants*, edited by Benjamin Birkinbine, Rodrigo García, and Janet Wasko, aims to summarizes this complex reality to a reader who may be not be very familiar, or who may be completely unfamiliar, with Grupo Prisa at all, since the largest amount of literature on the group has been published in Spanish. Thus, the main goal of this volume is to introduce to an English audience a concise history of one of the most influential and largest multimedia conglomerates of the Spanish-speaking world with a significant presence in Latin America. In spite of its corporate decline, today Grupo Prisa can still declare itself "the world's leading Spanish- and Portuguese-language media group in the creation and distribution of content in the fields of culture, education, news and information, and entertainment". The products and services of the company are still present in 23 countries and the presence of the company in Brazil and Portugal, and among the growing Hispanic community in the United States, opens up a global market of 700 million people.

Through this book, the readers will get access to the history of a media conglomerate that has gone through its 40th anniversary in the midst of a substantial corporate and professional crisis. The history begins after the death of dictator Francisco Franco (1892–1975) and develops accompanying the restoration of democracy in Spain, a period in which Grupo Prisa went from developing outstanding brands with an international presence such as *El País* (newspaper), Los 40 (musical radio), Santillana (educational content and services), W Radio (radio, Colombia), or *As* (sports newspaper) to a very painful process of divestment and corporate contraction.

To this end, and in addition to the company's history, the book will focus on the processes of concentration, internationalization, and financialization carried out by the group since the beginning of this century. In Chapter 2, a historical account is provided with a concise chronicle of the company. In this chapter key historical moments are highlighted taking into account the social, political, and economic context in which they take place. In Chapter 3,

Introduction 7

we provide the financial profile of the company. This chapter provides details on financial data and market share, corporate structure and properties, and strategies and new developments. In Chapter 4, the political economy profile of Grupo Prisa is addressed, including ownership, ties to the state and lobbying efforts, boards of directors and interlockings, and labour and social marketing issues. In Chapter 5, a cultural profile of Prisa discusses the symbolic universe and ideology of the company, its contribution to popular products and services and to the building of everyday life for millions of citizens, and its cultural exports and imports. The volume ends with brief concluding remarks on the company's power and significance.

The authors of this volume believe that the book will be useful for a large array of audiences, including scholars working within the fields of global media studies, international communication, media industries, or political economy of communication, as well as conceptually related fields like economics, sociology, international relations, or political science. In addition, the relatively shorter length and in-depth detail of the book may make it beneficial for students, graduate students, professors, or policymakers who have an interest in the development of one of the most important media conglomerates in the Spanish-speaking world. Consequently, the book may work as supplemental material for courses focused on media industries and information technology, in particular, and economics, politics, or cultural studies, more broadly.

Bibliography

Albornoz, L.A. (2016). "Grupo Prisa," in Birkinbine, B., Gómez, R. and Wasko, J. (Eds.): *Global Media Giants*. New York: Routledge, pp. 206–225.
Almiron, N. (2010). *Journalism in Crisis: Corporate Media and Financialization*. Cresskill, NJ: Hampton Press.
———. (2018). "'Go and Get'em!' Authoritarianism, Elitism and Media in the Catalan Crisis," *The Political Economy of Communication*, 6(2): 39–73.
Cabrera, M. (2015). *Jesús de Polanco*. Barcelona: Galaxia Gutenberg.
EL PAÍS (2003). "Muere el editor José Manuel Lara, fundador del imperio editorial Planeta," *El País*, May 12.
Fernández-Quijada, D. and Arboledas, L. (2013). "The Clientelistic Nature of Television Policies in Democratic Spain," *Mass Communication & Society*, 16(2): 200–221.
Hallin, D. and Mancini, P. (2004). *Comparing Media Systems: Three Models of Media and Politics*. Cambridge, MA: Cambridge University Press.
Seoane, M.C. and Sueiro, S. (2004). *Una historia de El País y del Grupo Prisa*. Barcelona: Plaza y Janés.

2 History[1]

Based in Madrid, Grupo Prisa has managed in the last decades to consolidate its Ibero-American reach, and at the beginning of 2020 its products and services reach more than 60 million potential users in 22 countries. Its most prominent assets include *El País*, Spain's leading newspaper, self-proclaimed as "the global newspaper" (with an English edition and editions for Latin America, Brazil, and Catalonia); Grupo Santillana, a group of publishing houses producing books in Spanish, Portuguese, French, and English; and, Prisa Radio, the world's largest Spanish-language radio group, with a presence in thirteen countries, including all major Hispanic markets.

However, since the mid-2000s, Prisa has faced its most difficult time, as it has been saddled with bank debt in excess of five billion euros, against a backdrop of widespread economic crisis in its traditional and core market, Spain. In response to this situation, Prisa management has pursued a strategy of debt restructuring, divestments, layoffs, and a search for new investors. As a result, the multimedia conglomerate has experienced profound changes in its shareholding structure and its presence in various cultural industries. The equity shares of the Jesús Polanco family plunged from 71 per cent in 2009 to less than 10 per cent in 2014, while a number of financial institutions and hedge funds have gained prominence. Severely impacted by the international economic crisis that seriously affected Spain in 2009 and by poor management decisions, this process was coupled with a decline in Prisa's presence in certain industries previously considered its core business, notably its audiovisual division. In fact, Grupo Prisa has been reporting losses every year since 2010.

According to Núria Almiron and Ana I. Segovia (2012), Prisa's corporate history can be divided into three main stages based on the expansion of the firm, which we will take as cornerstone years. First, we must consider the establishment of the company and its first steps with dozens of shareholders backing the project, from 1972 to 1983. Second, there is the period of growth

Grupo Prisa undertook from 1983, the year that marks the control of the firm by the Polanco family and the kick-off of its cross-media and international expansion. That brings us, finally, to a phase that begins in 2007, characterized by a perfect storm of events of a different nature – the international capitalist crisis, the death of Jesús Polanco (1929–2007), the advance of the digital revolution and its implications – which drove Prisa to a profound breaking point that took the company to half its size (and a third of its revenues) when compared with its glory days.

As we will discuss in the final chapter of this book, we consider that a new stage can be envisioned after the new major shareholder, the hedge fund Amber Capital, took control of Grupo Prisa and Juan Luis Cebrián was finally removed from all relevant positions within the company as of the first day of 2018. In 2019, it seemed that Prisa was taking its first steps to refocus intently in two main areas – media and education – while divesting completely from television broadcasting.

Early Years (1972–1983)

The origins of Grupo Prisa go back to January 1972, when five personalities of Spanish society – José Ortega Spottorno (son of philosopher José Ortega y Gasset, director of *Revista de Occidente*, and managing director of Alianza Editorial), Carlos Mendo (journalist), Darío Valcárcel (journalist), Juan José de Carlos (lawyer), and Ramón Jordán de Urríes (aristocrat) – established the company Promotora de Informaciones S.A. (PRISA). Additionally, they registered a new newspaper brand, *El País*, which went into circulation in 1976 when the Spanish government that took over after the death of dictator Francisco Franco (1892–1975) granted its authorization.

The first issue of *El País*, a leading daily in the Spanish language and key player in journalism in the Spanish-speaking world, appeared on May 4, 1976, after more than four years fighting the Francoist bureaucracy.[2] It was a newspaper defining itself as an independent, a high-quality morning newspaper, with a European vocation, and whose editorials and news-gathering practices have been considered an authoritative and professional standard since its beginning.[3] *El País* – a morning paper that "presented itself as a liberal, quality and independent newspaper and never hid the influence of the once prominent Orteguian newspaper *El Sol* (1917–1939) and the British newspaper *The Times*" (Sanmartí, 2018: 190) – was the backbone, symbolically and monetarily speaking, of the multimedia company that developed during the next decades. In fact, once operating, the newspaper was profitable by 1977 (0.25 million euros earnings before taxes); by 1983, the earnings before taxes were multiplied by fifteen, reaching 3.7 million euros.

10 History

The early years were also marked by a series of internal struggles in Grupo Prisa, which went from five shareholders to 1,096 in 1977 (Seoane and Sueiro, 2004). Most of them were part of the intellectual, academic, or politically liberal complex close to the transition process in Spain, and no one held more than 7.5 per cent of the shareholding structure of *El País* when it began publishing.[4] By 1975, Jesús Polanco was CEO of the company, and chairperson in 1984, when he already had 40 per cent control of Prisa (Polanco gained a majority of shares in 1983 through a cohort of collaborators, including other members of his family).[5]

During the transition from the authoritarian Francoist regime to a full-fledged democracy, *El País* demonstrated its commitment to young democracy after the coup d'état attempt on Monday, February 23, 1981 (known in Spain as 23-F, and also known as the Tejerazo), which took place only 43 months after the first free general elections were held after Franco's death. Lieutenant-Colonel Antonio Tejero led 200 armed Civil Guard officers into the Congress of Deputies during the vote to elect Leopoldo Calvo-Sotelo as Prime Minister.[6] The officers held the parliamentarians and ministers hostage for 18 hours, during which time King Juan Carlos I denounced the coup in a televised address, calling for rule of law and the democratic government to continue. *El País* published a 16-page special edition with a cover story entitled "El País, con la Constitución" (see Chapter 5).

The prestige gained by *El País* in its first years of operation was also helped by strict compliance with journalistic standards and the fact that it was the first newspaper in Spain to establish internal quality control standards. It was also the first Spanish newspaper to create the figure of *el defensor del lector* (equivalent to the press ombudsman) and to write and publish a style book (the first edition of which was published in 1977) that became a reference in the world of journalism written in Spanish. On the other hand, the publisher of *El País* established several early collaboration agreements with other European newspapers with a social-democratic line. Thus, for example, in the late 1980s it participated in the creation of a common network of information resources with *La Repubblica* (Italy) and *Le Monde* (France).

The newspaper furthermore openly supported the Spanish Socialist Workers' Party (PSOE) since the early 1980s, and this support became a constant feature of the media group in the following decades of socialist governments, from Felipe González's terms of office (1982–1996) to those of José Luis Rodríguez Zapatero (2004–2011).[7] This was an alliance that helped Grupo Prisa to develop its cross-media expansion in the 1980s and 1990s and provided a perfect example of "media-political clientelism", as defined by David Fernández-Quijada and Luis Arboledas (2013). Nonetheless, this well-oiled relationship with government leaders was not a new strategy for Jesús Polanco, who built his editorial empire from textbooks through the foundation of the Santillana firm (created in 1960 and 40 years later incorporated into Grupo Prisa) thanks to the political ties with the Francoist regime in Spain,[8] or the political regimes in Latin America during his 1960s and 1970s expansion, which included both democratic regimes and dictatorships.[9] In fact, it should be noted that in the 1960s Santillana was more prosperous in Latin America than in Spain.

Regarding Santillana, which specialized in the educational sector (dissemination of manuals, literacy and vocational training primers, and books for children and young people), it is worth noting that the company gradually entered the field of fiction and literature in the 1980s by acquiring prestigious publishing labels such as Alfaguara (founded in 1964 under the direction of the late Nobel laureate Camilo José Cela, joined Santillana in 1980) and Aguilar (created in 1923, joined Santillana in 1986).

Cross-Media Expansion (1984–2007)

In 1984 Grupo Prisa carried out its first statute changes, which transformed its corporate purposes, expanded the scope to the management and exploitation of any mass media, as well as the participation in any mercantile act or the partnership with other companies, whatever their corporate purpose (Seoane and Sueiro, 2004). That was the keystone that enabled the newly appointed chairman Jesús Polanco to start a process of intense business growth that allowed the company to emerge as the main multimedia group in Spain in the 1990s, even as it remained just a newspaper publisher until 1983.

In 1983, Prisa launched an unsuccessful small radio network called Radio El País. However, the business turned out to be not as prosperous as anticipated (it closed in 1987), which justified the acquisition of Cadena SER, Spain's leading radio network in terms of audience share. The acronym SER stands for Sociedad Española de Radiodifusión, which translates to the Spanish Broadcasting Company in English.[10] The radio network is remembered in Spain for the role played by Radio Madrid, one of its main stations, during the failed coup d'état led by Antonio Tejero on 23-F in 1981. With the Congress of Deputies taken over by the coup plotters, the employees of the Cadena SER continued their live broadcast with open microphones from within the Congress of Deputies, which meant that the general public was able to follow along by radio as events unfolded. As such, the dawn of February 23–24, 1981, is remembered as the "night of transistors".[11]

The acquisition of Cadena SER was a sure bet, as it was already a successful radio network with a good number of owned and operated stations as part of the business. Realizing its growth in this area would have been extremely difficult, Prisa eventually bought the company through a series of acquisitions, beginning with the acquisition of minor shares in 1984. After successive share purchases and a capital increase operation in 1986, Prisa took control of 71 per cent of the shareholding.[12] The takeover of Cadena SER is the starting point of Prisa's growth, from publisher to radiobroadcaster to television broadcasting, as the opportunities in the Spanish media market were encouraging the development of the private media sector.[13]

In 1988, *El País*' editor in chief, Juan Luis Cebrián, became Prisa's CEO, when the company started a process of cross-media expansion at vertical, horizontal, and diagonal levels (Doyle, 2002). In fact, the statutes of Grupo Prisa were reformed again in 1989, at the same time that the company transformed into a holding company, solidifying the intention of expansion to other areas of business, as well as the opening to the process of financialization – including the participation in the capital and monetary markets (PRISA, 1989: 1, article 2, letter f).

Under Cebrián's direction, Prisa intensively invested in the national and international markets until 2008, increasing its activities not only to the radio business, but also to television (including pay-TV as well as local and national free-to-air television), magazines, printing, advertising, and music and book publishing (by taking over the activities of Grupo Santillana in 2000). The holding company went public in 2000, with 20 per cent of its capital, and it reached the selective IBEX 35, the Madrid Stock Exchange, for some years. As we will see, Prisa expanded, building a multimedia empire in the Spanish- and Portuguese-language markets, with some attempts at penetration into the European markets, too.

From the mid-1980s to the mid-2000s, Grupo Prisa diversified vertically in the printing and distribution business, and horizontally in the publishing business. In 1987 Prisa established its magazine branch (PROGRESA, which is now integrated in the publishing house El País), which included the news magazine *El Globo* (1987);[14] *Claves de la razón práctica*, a philosophy journal launched in 1990 directed by anti-Franco political analyst Javier Pradera (1934–2011) and philosopher Fernando Savater (1947–); *Cinemanía* (cinema news, created in 1995 and sold in 2015); and *El gran musical* (musical news magazine, relaunched by Prisa in 1991 and shut down in 1995).

In 1996 Prisa also acquired a business newspaper, *Cinco Días* (buying it in different steps), and 75 per cent of *As* (sports newspaper).

During the 1990s Prisa participated in various European newspapers, a project that lasted for some years in most cases. For example, it was part of the British *The Independent* from 1990 to 1998, the Portuguese *Público* from 1992 to 1997, and the Mexican *La Prensa* from 1993 to 1996. At the end of the twentieth century, Prisa would also embark in the regional press business in Spain, creating a joint venture with another eight regional Spanish newspapers (*Canarias 7*, *Diario de Avisos*, *Diario de Burgos*, *Diario Palentino*,

History 13

El Punt, Gaceta Regional de Salamanca, La Voz de Almería, and Segre) to manage a new company, Gestión de Medios de Prensa (GMP), owned 51 per cent by Prisa. However, GMP was liquidated in February 2014 (PRISA, 2014) when Grupo Prisa was in the middle of its divestment process.

Prisa's expansion would even reach the Bolivian press, creating in 2000 three joint ventures with Grupo Garáfulic, including the dailies *La Razón* – the leader in Bolivia, *El Nuevo Día*, *Extra*, the free-to-air television station ATB, and an Internet business. By 2003, the association with Garáfulic disappeared, leaving Prisa with total control of the enterprises, which would be exchanged for 12 per cent of the US television company V-me in 2009 (see more in the next section).

Finally, the only current addition to the press business area was the acquisition of 15 per cent of the French newspaper *Le Monde* in 2005 (see Table 3.1 in Chapter 3 for a summary of the operations) – 20 per cent today due to the capital increase of Le Monde Libre Société Commandité Simple (PRISA, 2018). Meanwhile, the latest news in some publications of the French and Spanish press reported an agreement between the stockholders to facilitate the exit of Prisa from the company.

Regarding the diagonal expansion of Prisa to other media segments, the first incursion was, as mentioned, in the radio business. In 1986, Prisa acquired a majority part of the Spanish radio network Cadena SER. Then, in 1992, Prisa closed an agreement with Grupo Godó to buy Antena 3 Radio,[15] creating a new company called Sociedad de Servicios Radiofónicos Unión Radio, which is 80 per cent owned by Prisa and 20 per cent by Godó. This purchase attracted a lot of criticism, given that Antena 3 Radio was politically anti-PSOE (in government from 1982 until 1996), while Cadena SER was just the opposite, and because it infringed the ownership concentration regulation in the radio sector at the time (Segovia, 2005).

The merger triggered a lawsuit against the consent granted by the socialist government, and a legal ruling by the Spanish Supreme Court in 2000 annulled the agreement, which was subsequently appealed to the Constitutional Court. In the end, Prisa lost the petition. Nonetheless, the ruling was never executed, and in 2005 the new socialist government led by José Luis Rodríguez Zapatero (2004–2011) made changes in the legislation, which finally gave the go-ahead to the concentration process.[16]

On the topic of the diversification strategies, it is also noteworthy that, at the end of 1999, Prisa created a new company, Gran Vía Musical (GVM), by integrating five businesses related to the music industry – from recording to distribution, including publishing and production of live entertainment. The goal was to become the first Spanish multinational in Latin music, attracting artists from different countries and musical styles, and extending the Latin and Spanish music market. In 2002, the expansion to Latin America began with the opening of an office in Mexico. However, months later, the music sector started its recession due to piracy and Internet downloads of music recordings and the restructuring of the industry took a toll on Prisa as well. In 2004, Prisa reported an agreement with Universal Music Group to sell its record production assets (Muxxic, Horus, and Eurotropical), including the permission to use Prisa's music brands, such as "Los números uno de 40" or the albums of Máxima FM (radio network). So the company took a step aside in the field of music production and marketing, while maintaining its activities in the area of concert planning (Planet Events),[17] music publishing (Nova and Lyrics & Music), and DVD and CD commercialization (GVM Colecciones) (El PAÍS, 2004).

The arrival of Grupo Prisa in the television sector came in 1989, after the socialist government granted the company one of the three private television channels created with the passage of new legislation in 1988. The Private Television Act 10/1988 caused an unprecedented upheaval in the television sector in Spain, given that it meant the end of the public monopoly, which had been in place since the arrival of Televisión Española (the public broadcaster) in 1956. The only transformation to the television landscape was the coming of regional public broadcasters from 1983 onwards. The 1988 Act implied the arrival of private broadcasters and the "liberalization" of the television industry.

Prisa was ready to take part in the television business as it had created Sogetel (Sociedad General de Televisión) in 1984. Sociedad de Televisión Canal Plus, a joint venture with Canal+ France and other financial investors (Spanish financial entities such as Banco Bilbao Vizcaya, Banesto, Bankinter, Caja Madrid, and Banca March), was also established in 1989. Then, in 1996, the audio-visual division of Prisa was renamed Sogecable, to accommodate Canal+ and Canal Satélite Digital (CSD).

Canal+, a pay-TV channel, began broadcasting in 1990, which was followed by a new wave of criticism. It made no sense, arguably, that the opening of the Spanish television market was burdened by a pay-TV channel when there were other free-to-air contestants, along with the two successful bidders, Gestevisión and Antena 3 de Televisión (Giordano and Zeller, 1999; Pérez Gómez, 2002). Finally, the peculiarity of the choice made by the government led by Felipe González (PSOE) compelled Canal+ to broadcast six hours of its programming each day free-to-air.[18]

Oddly enough, this partially pay-TV channel converted in 2005 into a fully free-to-air channel named Cuatro. By then the company sensed that it was time to open up this television segment, given that its pay-TV service would be filled by its new satellite television provider, CSD, that started operating in 1997. CSD merged with another satellite television service provider, Vía Digital, creating Digital+ in 2002. This merger is notable because it is the point of origin of the exponential debt that would drag Prisa to the divestment process described in the next section (see also Chapter 3 for a more detailed account).

In order to understand this back and forth process within the pay-TV and the free-to-air television segments, we must explain the stakes at play in the Spanish political and economic context. Grupo Prisa has always been characterized by its comfortable relationship with the socialist government led by Felipe González, in power until 1996. First, as explained, Prisa was between the bidders in the first public tender for private television channels, and it was awarded one of the three television licences. Then, in 1995, the Telecommunications by Satellite Act liberalized the television via satellite sector, and two companies were ready to enter the competition: CSD, part of Grupo Prisa, backed by Canal+ France (then Vivendi Group), and Vía Digital, a firm led by Telefónica with other investors (including the Spanish public broadcaster Radio Television Española, the Mexican group Televisa, and some Spanish regional public broadcasters and press companies). However, both CSD and Vía Digital were longing for football broadcasting rights. Considering the importance of this sport in Spain, broadcasts of football matches, along with the premieres of Hollywood blockbusters, will always be the cornerstone to any pay-TV service in the country. This was the beginning of what is known as the football wars, also branded as the set-top box wars, where the courts intervened more than once, as explained further on.

At the end of 1994 Jesús Polanco entered into an agreement with the owner of the football broadcasting rights that Prisa did not hold, Antonio Asensio,[19] and created a joint venture, Audiovisual Sport (AVS), igniting the so-called first football war between the two satellite platforms.[20] Meanwhile, it became evident that the new party in government, Partido Popular (Spanish centre-right), wished to promote a new big media group to counterbalance Prisa's influence on Spanish media. In this context, the national telecommunications company Telefónica, in the middle of its privatization process, seemed an excellent choice: its CEO, Juan Villalonga, was a close friend of then President José María Aznar. After the pact between Polanco and Asensio, the business opportunities of Vía Digital decreased radically, so the Spanish government passed a regulation that interfered with CSD hampering the distribution of the set-top boxes (cable boxes) used by the satellite provider.[21] Furthermore, there were other administrative and legislative interventions driven by the government to meddle with the development of CSD (Segovia, 2005).

Nevertheless, CSD (Grupo Prisa) and Vía Digital (Telefónica) lost more than 1.365 billion euros (Rosique, 2012) from 1997 to 2001, so it looked like the merger of both satellite platforms, creating Digital+, was inevitable. There were not enough consumers in the Spanish market to sustain two companies, given the small inclination of Spanish television viewers to pay for the service. So this integration into Digital+, branded under the control of Sogecable, became a reality in 2003. As a result of this operation, Telefónica owned 22.2 per cent of Sogecable, while Prisa held 16.4 per cent. As Sogecable was a public company since 1999, Grupo Prisa increased its control, buying stock in the following years. In fact, by 2007 Prisa already held more than 50 per cent of Sogecable's shares, facing the obligation to launch a takeover bid. In total, 3.9 billion euros were needed for the merger with Vía Digital in 2003, and the total acquisition of Sogecable in 2007 (see Chapter 3).

Thus, the takeover of Sogecable was the beginning of the end of the participation of Prisa in the television sector. During this period Prisa's tentacles reached free-to-air television, after the transformation of Canal+ into Cuatro in 2005; pay-TV, with Digital+; and the local television segment, with Localia TV. This local television network began operating in 2000 in Madrid, and reached 75 stations by the end of 2003. Nonetheless, Localia TV only brought losses to the company, and it closed in December 2008. From 2006 to 2008, Prisa's debt soared, surpassing 5 billion euros.

In regard to the publishing sector, Santillana – along with its printing division, Mateu Cromo Artes Gráficas, and its advertising sales division, Gerencia de Medios – integrated into Grupo Prisa in 2000 just before the holding went public. In 2001, Santillana purchased the Brazilian Editora Moderna,[22] and in 2016 the Colombian Grupo Editorial Norma (Carvajal Soluciones Educativas).[23] Despite such acquisitions, Santillana has been characterized in its history as expanding its reach in Latin America on its own.

In fact, this ability to replicate its business across the Atlantic in other Spanish-speaking countries was useful to the internationalization of Prisa's radio sector in the twenty-first century, given that it centred in the same region. This process began in 1999, when Prisa acquired 19 per cent of Radio Caracol, a Colombian radio company, which paved the way to shape Grupo Latino de Radio (GLR), the Prisa radio division in Latin America. GLR was created in 1999 with 50 per cent Prisa participation, obtaining total control of the company in 2004.[24] That same year the Spanish group bought 50 per cent of Radiópolis, a Mexican commercial radio station owned by Televisa, which ranked in fifth place in that country. Then in 2004 it purchased Radio Continental and Radio Estéreo in Argentina; and, in 2006, obtained Iberoamericana Radio Chile, the main Chilean radio group. By then, GLR was rooted in some of the most important Latin American radio markets.

Consequently, in the area of radio, by 2007 Unión Radio was the most important radio group in Spanish, with more than 22 million listeners and 1,250 radio stations (owned and operated) distributed across Spain, the United States, Mexico, Colombia, Costa Rica, Panama, Argentina, and Chile (PRISA, 2008). According to Prisa's annual report, 20 per cent of the EBITDA of its income

History 17

came from international operations, and the radio segment (14.83 per cent) was almost as profitable as the education (15.38 per cent) and press (17.54 per cent) areas.

It is worth noting that by 2007 a small amount of the EBITDA (0.23 per cent) corresponded to Prisa's digital operating segment, which gathered the various websites of the company trademarks: ElPais.com, CadenaSER.com, CincoDías.com, As.com, Los40.com, Cuatro.com, Plus.es, SantillanaEnRed.com, Kalipedia.com, ParaSaber.com, and ClasificadosElPais.com. The division in charge of the digital area of Prisa was Prisacom, created in 2000. It is worth noting that Prisacom decided to introduce the pay-walled service of the online edition of *El País* in 2002, after six years online free of charge (since May 1996). This business strategy was not successful, and by mid-2005 the version went back to free access. Just the same path travelled by *The New York Times* (Albornoz, 2007: 154–156).

The core business segment of Grupo Prisa by 2007 was the audio-visual division, which was responsible for 51 per cent of the EBITDA. Adding to the free-to-air television channel Cuatro and the satellite pay-TV CSD in Spain, Prisa purchased the Portuguese media conglomerate Grupo Media Capital (free-to-air television and radio), controlling 94.4 per cent in 2007, with the focus of expanding these business areas into a much bigger Portuguese market: Brazil. However, this incursion into Brazilian territory was never accomplished.

It should be noted that Grupo Media Capital is the largest communication and entertainment group in Portugal, with a strong presence in the main segments of communication and production of audio-visual material. In television, the company has TVI, the leading television channel in Portugal, as well as TVI24 (news), TVI Fiction, TVI International, TVI Reality, and TVI Africa. In radio, it owns one of the most prestigious and transverse national radio groups: Media Capital Radio (MCR), which includes Rádio Comercial, the audience leader; M80 Rádio; Cidade; Smooth FM; Vodafone FM; and the online radio website Cotonete. Media Capital also has the Media Capital Digital division, whose main asset is IOL, a multimedia content provider (also an Internet service provider previously). In the audio-visual production sector, Plural Entertainment is one of the largest producers on the Iberian Peninsula, particularly in the areas of Portuguese fiction and Spanish entertainment.

Grupo Prisa paid a high price for its pre-eminence in the audio-visual sector. The total acquisition of Sogecable and the control of pay-TV that came with it took place in 2007, just a few months after the international economic crisis started to cause major disruptions in the Spanish market. According to Prisa's CEO at the time, Juan Luis Cebrián (2008), who spoke to the shareholders at the 2008 Extraordinary Meeting, Prisa spent 6.19 billion euros in acquisitions from 2000 to 2008. In 2007, Sogecable was valued at 3.87 billion euros, or 27.98 euros per share. When Prisa parted with the pay-TV company, it received a total amount of only 1.7 billion euros.[25]

18 *History*

The fall of Grupo Prisa began then, with the massive debt obtained before the economic crisis; it deepened with the demise of Jesús Polanco, Prisa's creator and head officer for more than two decades, in July 2007, and it was unsurmountable due to the changes coming to the communications sector.

Crisis, Divestments, and Refocus (2008–)

As we will discuss further in Chapter 3, which focuses on the economic profile and corporate strategies of Grupo Prisa, the root of its financial problems lies in what was until 2013 the main audio-visual asset: Sogecable (CSD). From this date on, Prisa's trend of expansion completely reversed, shifting to contraction and divestment. Financial problems led the company to make substantial changes in its strategy and structure (as well as in ownership, discussed later in Chapter 4), with the disposal of some of its more valuable assets or parts of the more profitable properties and the closing of the less lucrative ones.

The years 2008 and 2009 are a paradigmatic example of the process Prisa suffered in order to renegotiate its gigantic financial debt. The positive balance of 83 million euros in the company's net profit in 2008 resulted from the 300 million euros obtained from the sale of the head offices of Cadena SER, *El País*, and Radio Barcelona. In addition to this, the year began with an agreement to gradually sell more than 16 per cent of the radio business (Unión Radio) to the hedge fund 3i Group plc and ended with the local television network, Localia TV, closing its operations in December. Furthermore, in 2009 Prisa closed its bookstores, called Crisol, sold 25 per cent of Grupo Santillana to the investment fund DLJ South American Partners LC, and began dismantling its audio-visual sector.

At the end of 2009, the international economic crisis took a heavy toll on Spain. The economic recession hit the consumer market, and the advertising market fell 21.9 per cent (after an 11.4 per cent decrease in 2008). This situation occurred simultaneously with the expansion of digital terrestrial television (DTT) (in Spain, the analogue television switch-off took place in April 2010) and prompted the passing of two regulations that greatly impacted the Spanish television landscape. First, the Aznar government (PP) opened up the process of concentration between DTT broadcasters when it allowed a television company to broadcast up to eight channels. Second, advertising was eliminated from the national public television channels, allowing private broadcasters to absorb this portion of the commercial market.[26]

The modification of the legislation allowed Grupo Prisa to close a deal with Gestevisión Telecinco, controlled by then Italian Prime Minister Silvio Berlusconi, to merge its free-to-air channel, Cuatro, with Telecinco (and its corresponding secondary channels settled with the developing of DTT)

History 19

through a share swap that resulted in a new company: Mediaset España, with a 17.34 per cent ownership interest by Prisa. The goal of this new company was always evident: to make money selling the shares afterwards to pay off debt. Indeed, Prisa disposed of its shares between 2014 and 2015, which earned the company almost 845 million euros in total (PRISA, 2015).

Regarding Prisa's pay-TV business, as stated earlier, in December 2009 the company sold 44 per cent of Digital+ for 976 million euros to Mediaset España and Telefónica.

Nevertheless, Prisa didn't completely stop acquiring new assets, which suggests that its expansion plans in America were not entirely put aside. In 2009 the company acquired several shares of V-me Media, a US television network broadcasting only in Spanish. It reached a share peak of 48.28 per cent in 2012, but in 2013 Prisa sold almost all of them, retaining only 3.9 per cent, which means the company abandoned Prisa's perimeter of consolidation (PRISA, 2013).

The losses, however, have grown more visible and more severe since 2010. Triggered by the negotiation of the giant debt, financial entities took over Grupo Prisa, causing the bad debts to become capital. Furthermore, new shareholders joined in through the company's capital expansion and the restructuring of the financial debt. Liberty Acquisitions Holdings, a special-purpose acquisition company, incorporated into Prisa in 2010, leaving the Polanco family and its closest partners with 30 per cent of the firm. The remaining 70 per cent went public and were mostly held by institutional investors. Almost a decade afterwards, the Polanco family retains less than 10 per cent interest in the company (see Chapter 4 for a more detailed account regarding ownership).

This ownership turmoil took a toll on the editorial staff of Prisa's flagship information outlets: *El País* and Cadena SER. Many valuable and historical journalists and collaborators have abandoned the pages of *El País* because the newspaper publisher has turned towards a journalism more attached to the interests of the investor groups (especially since the debt crisis) than to quality journalism. And many sectors of the left wing ideological spectrum see *El País* as a bourgeois publication that forms part of Spain's dominant political-economic establishment.

Meanwhile, on the business side, in early 2013, the dismantling of the Prisa Digital division began, which put an end to an integrated digital strategy that included the creation of a platform that served as a repository for the archive of all of the company's media. The ambitious plan "has dissolved for different reasons, including the lack of clear direction, the complexity of the group, its growing lack of resources and the country's recessive context" (Carmona, 2013). The difficulty of monetizing digital content is a recurring one and Prisa is present in markets where consumers are reluctant to pay for content.

The financial losses that began relatively slowly in 2010, with losses of 35 million euros, soared to more than 1 billion euros in 2013, and doubled to total losses amounting to 2.310 billion euros in 2014. During that period, Grupo Prisa continued its efforts in cost control (6,522 jobs were lost between 2008 and 2015; see Chapter 4) and the execution of its debt reduction plan to attain a sustainable debt level (in 2014 it managed to reduce the financial debt to under the three billion euro threshold), while preserving Prisa's core assets. By then, the core assets were the radio and education divisions (not television). This context explains why the company reached an agreement in November 2013 with 3i Group plc to buy back its Prisa Radio shares on a five-year instalment plan that was completed in February 2019. This allowed the company to return to its previous situation in which 80 per cent was owned by Grupo Prisa and the remaining 20 per cent by Grupo Godó. In addition, it reached a deal in the first four months of 2019 to repurchase the 25 per cent of Santillana that Prisa sold in 2009 in order to regain 100 per cent of the company.

Moreover, Prisa's interest in the publishing sector has leaned increasingly towards the education area since the company sold Santillana Ediciones Generales to Bertelsmann in 2014 (the book publishing business). At the same time, it has been increasing its hold in the Latin American education-publishing sector and expanding these activities towards a digital transformation, which includes the provision of subscription models for learning systems. For the moment, this move is providing a solid advance.

Meanwhile, since the mid-2010s, Prisa has been trying to eliminate its participation in the television and audio-visual production segments. The last transaction closed by Prisa with Telefónica, a deal approved by the country's competition watchdog, the National Commission on Markets and Competition (CNMC), took place in May 2015. As already noted, Prisa sold a 56 per cent share in Digital+ to Telefónica for 706.8 million euros, a quantity that tripled the amount spent three years before by Prisa to purchase a similar equity share. It is worth noting that in 2013 Canal+'s revenues – then owned by Grupo Prisa, Telefónica Contenidos, and Mediaset España – amounted to 1.166 billion euros, which explains Prisa's revenues falling from 2.726 billion euros in 2013 to 1.455 billion euros in 2014, when Canal+ was no longer associated with Prisa.

As a result, Prisa TV, the audio-visual holding company in charge of content production, acquisition, and management of audio-visual, publishing, and distribution rights for television channels, marketing, and customer management, ceased to exist in 2013 (PRISA, 2013).

Furthermore, the company tried to get rid of Grupo Media Capital, its last property in the television and audio-visual production business, on more than one occasion. First, in 2011, Prisa sold 10 per cent of Media Capital to Miguel Pais do Amaral (oddly enough, the original founder of the company) with the intent of increasing the participation of this Portuguese businessman in the coming years. As this did not happen, Prisa exercised its right to buy back the 10 per cent in 2013. Then, in 2017, Prisa sold Media Capital to the French media and telecommunications group Altice NV for 440 million euros, pending the approval of the Portuguese competition watchdog. However, in 2018 the AdC (Competition Authority) decided against the acquisition, given the large presence of the French group in the Portuguese market after its purchase of Portugal Telecom in 2015 (now Altice Portugal).

Finally, in September 2019, Grupo Prisa announced the agreement to sell Media Capital to the Portuguese media group Cofina. The transaction needed multiple approvals, from the AdC as well as some of the Prisa's debtholders and the General Assembly. However, at the last moment Cofina backed out of the purchase pleading economic difficulties.[27] If the sale would had taken place, it would have meant the complete withdrawal of the company from the television and audio-visual production business and the abandonment of the Portuguese market.

In conclusion, Prisa is beginning to position itself solely as an education and information company, thereby strengthening its current core business. However, its financial position at the beginning of 2020 is still on a tightrope: net income in 2018 was still in the red (–237 million euros), and the first three trimesters of 2019 did not get much better (–110.4 million euros). If the sale of Media Capital would had gone through, it would have reasonably reduced the financial debt (still estimated at more than 1 billion euros). The silver lining is that 20 per cent of the revenues in 2019 came from digital businesses (LA VANGUARDIA, 2019) and the numbers of online students and advertising digital sales are growing steadily.[28]

Notes

1. Some of the ideas in Chapter 2 come from the chapter dedicated to Grupo Prisa in *Global Media Giants*, written by Luis A. Albornoz in Birkinbine *et al.* (2016); the article "Financialization, Economic Crisis, and Corporate Strategies in Top Media Companies: The Case of Grupo Prisa" (Almiron and Segovia, 2012); and Núria Alimiron's doctoral dissertation (2006) entitled *Poder financiero y poder mediático: banca y grupos de comunicación. Los casos del SCH y PRISA (1976–2004)*.
2. Strictly speaking, *El País* was not daily until 1982. In its first six years it was published from Tuesday to Sunday only.
3. *El País* became a referent of democratic Spain especially after the unsuccessful coup d'état of February 1981, publishing a special edition called "*El País*, con la Constitución", calling citizens to pledge allegiance to democracy.
4. Enrique Bustamante (1986) highlights 43 political personalities in Prisa's shareholding between 1981 and 1983.
5. The different paracorporate/shareholders agreements led by Jesús Polanco enabled him to control 72.5% of the company by 1992, maintaining this control even after the public offering in 2000. After going public, the Polanco family still controlled 68% of shares.

22 *History*

6. Leopoldo Calvo-Sotelo (1926–2008), belonging to the political party Unión del Centro Democrático (UCD), was the second president of the Spanish government (February 26, 1981–December 2, 1982) since the restoration of democracy.
7. It is important to mention the cooling of this partisan relationship in the last years of the Rodríguez Zapatero government, especially after the legislation changes regarding the broadcasting sector in 2009. The Royal Decree-Law 11/2009 of August 13, regulating the provision of digital terrestrial pay-TV services through conditional access for state concessions, opened the DTT to the pay-TV market, a measure that could damage Prisa's effective pay-TV monopoly with Digital+.
8. According to Jesús Cacho (1999), thanks to a leak, Jesús Polanco had access to privileged information about the incoming education reform of 1970, making it possible for Santillana to have the textbooks ready for distribution before anyone else. Interestingly enough, then Minister for Education José Luis Villar Palasí (1922–2012), who was in charge of the reform, would later be part of Prisa's board of directors.
9. See Balcarce (2018).
10. After the Spanish Civil War (1936–1939), Unión Radio, formally inaugurated by King Alfonso XIII in Madrid on June 17, 1925, was renamed Cadena SER.
11. Sound technician Mariano Revilla, who along with parliamentary chronicler Rafael Luis Díaz performed live coverage of the investiture of the new prime minister, had the ability to leave a sound line open in connection with Cadena SER studios in Madrid. In this way, the central newsroom knew part of what was occurring there. Although it was not possible to broadcast what was happening in the session room of the Chamber of Deputies, this audio signal served to make the radio experience its most intense night in the early hours of February 23–24, 1981. The news services of Cadena SER then began a deployment of special bulletins that incorporated the news received thanks to the open line in Congress. Thus, it was known on the radio before any other place that there had been no deaths after the assault.
12. It was in 1992 when the government of Felipe González (PSOE) decided to divest the state's share package in Cadena SER (25%) and Prisa took total control of the radio network. In this regard, Carlos Barrera (1995: 169) points out: "In 1975, during the León Herrera ministry, a legal provision forced private radio stations (the main one being, by far, Cadena SER) to give away 25% of their shares to the State for free. This regressive measure, already in the throes of the dictatorship, was intended to exercise a certain control over private broadcasting through ownership. What the minister could not have foreseen at the time was that only seven years later a socialist government would emerge in Spain, being able then to influence the radio network with that quarter of the total capital".
13. The public press managed by the Francoist regime was auctioned or closed, there were new licences for the radio industry, and the television sector opened to private competition some years later (Fernández and Santana, 2000).
14. *El Globo*, inspired by *Time Magazine*, lasted just over six months and resulted in significant losses for the company (Frattini and Colías, 1996: 122).
15. Antena 3 Radio (also known as Antena 3 de Radio) was a Spanish generalist radio station in operation from May 4, 1982, until June 17, 1994. It served as the basis for the creation of the television channel Antena 3 in 1989 and the conglomerate Atresmedia Corporación.
16. Soon after the PSOE returned to government in 2004, Law 10/2005 of June 14 on Urgent Measures for the Promotion of Digital Terrestrial Television, the

History 23

Liberalization of Cable Television, and the Promotion of Pluralism passed. Among other matters, it relaxed the regulation on radio ownership, allowing a single company to control as many as five radio stations in the same geographical area (or 50% of the radio stations), or one third of the stations in the Spanish territory. This was precisely the approval Prisa needed to take full control of Antena 3 Radio and create a new company called Unión Radio.
17. Grupo Prisa sold 60% of Planet Events to Live Nation in December 2018 (PRISA, 2018).
18. The contract for the provision of television services signed by Sociedad de TV Canal Plus with the Spanish government required this obligation (Alonso, 1999: 256).
19. Antonio Asensio (1947–2001) was the founder of Grupo Zeta. He was part of one of the companies (Univisión, along with the media mogul Rupert Murdoch) that was not successful in the television bidding process of 1989. However, in 1992 he finally entered the television sector, buying 25% of Antena 3 de Televisión, one of the then new television private operators, and taking control of it. Asensio controlled the broadcasting football rights of 25 clubs beginning in 1998, an agreement that took away the rights from the previous owners (Sogecable and the regional television public operators in the FORTA association). Sogecable-Prisa reacted by submitting an offer together with Tele 5, Televisión Española (TVE), and FORTA. The solution to the conflict between the two companies came with the so-called Christmas Eve pact, in which Sogecable, Antena 3 Televisión, and Televisió de Catalunya (the public broadcasting network of Catalonia) created Audiovisual Sport to jointly exploit the first and second division football rights. The president of this company was Asensio.
20. At that time, the broadcasting rights were managed by each football club individually. This changed in 2015 thanks to a regulation that centralized the operations. Since this first so-called football war, there have been other confrontations with rival companies, like the multimedia communications company Grupo Mediapro. There are unfinished court battles even today.
21. This regulation established that satellite service providers must agree on the set-top box system; if not, the system would be the one already chosen by Vía Digital (Telefónica), which was in fact different from the one adopted by CSD (Prisa).
22. Editora Moderna, headquartered in the city of São Paulo, has been publishing and distributing didactic books, support materials, and literature books since 1968. It is one of the leading publishers in the Brazilian market.
23. Norma, founded in 1960, is a publishing house headquartered in Cali (Colombia) that currently has a presence in Argentina, Chile, Colombia, Guatemala, Mexico, Peru, and Puerto Rico.
24. Grupo Prisa acquired 19% of Radio Caracol Colombia from Valores Bavaria in 1999, creating the holding GLR with Radio Caracol (50% per company). In 2004, Prisa took complete control of the holding (Almiron, 2006).
25. Mediaset España and Telefónica bought 22% of Digital+ each for 976 million euros in 2009; and Telefónica paid 725 million euros in 2014 for the remaining 56%.
26. The socialist government (PSOE) approved Royal Decree-Law 1/2009 on urgent measures in the field of telecommunications in February 2009, and Act 8/2009 on the financing of the Spanish Radio and Television Corporation (CRTVE) in August 2009. Both of them were later consolidated in Law 7/2010 of Audiovisual Communication in April 2010.

27. Prisa has announced that it will take legal actions against Cofina because of the breach of contract (EL PAÍS, 2020).
28. In 2018, the revenues from digital advertising rose to almost 70 million euros, from a total of 484 million euros, while as the education sector earned more than 21% from the digital education systems (134 million of a total amount of 579 million euros). For example, the digital advertising sales in the press division meant a 53% increase, compensating for the 11% decrease in off-line advertising sales (PRISA, 2018), and it represented 30% of the press division's total revenues as of September 2019 (PRISA, 2019).

Bibliography

Albornoz, L.A. (2007). *Periodismo digital: los grandes diarios en la red*. Buenos Aires: La Crujía Ediciones.

———. (2016). "Grupo Prisa," in Birkinbine, B., Gómez, R. and Wasko, J. (Eds.): *Global Media Giants*. New York: Routledge, pp. 206–225.

Almiron, N. (2006). *Poder financiero y poder mediático: banca y grupos de comunicación. Los casos del SCH y PRISA (1976–2004)*. Doctoral dissertation. Barcelona: Autonomous University of Barcelona.

Almiron, N. and Segovia, A. (2012). "Financialization, Economic Crisis, and Corporate Strategies in Top Media Companies: The Case of Grupo Prisa," *International Journal of Communication*, 6: 2894–2917.

Alonso González, F. (1999). *Sogecable descodificado: cifras y claves empresariales de Canal+ en España*. Madrid: Fragua.

Balcarce, L. (2018). *Prisa: liquidación de existencias*. Madrid: Ediciones Akal.

Barrera, C. (1995). *Periodismo y franquismo: De la censura a la apertura*. Barcelona: Ediciones Internacionales Universitarias.

Birkinbine, B., Gómez, R. and Wasko, J. (Eds.) (2016). *Global Media Giants*. New York: Routledge.

Bustamante, E. (1986). "El País: Análisis del poder," in Imbert, G. and Vidal Beneyto, J. (Eds.): *El País o la referencia dominante*. Barcelona: Mitre, pp. 55–107.

Cacho, J. (1999). *El negocio de la libertad*. Madrid: Foca.

Carmona, J. (2013). "Prisa desmantela su división digital, su apuesta estrella, tras incumplir objetivos y quedarse sin recursos," *Capital Madrid*, March 1.

Cebrián, J.L. (2008). *Prisa's Chief Executive Officer Statement: Extraordinary Shareholders'*. General Meeting, Madrid, Spain, December 5.

Doyle, G. (2002). *Media Ownership*. London: Sage Publications.

EL PAÍS (2004). "PRISA vende a Universal su producción discográfica," *El País*, April 15.

EL PAÍS (2020). "PRISA emprenderá acciones contra Cofina por anular la compra de Media Capital," *El País*, March 11.

Fernández, I. and Santana, F. (2000). *Estado y medios de comunicación en la España democrática*. Madrid: Alianza Editorial.

Fernández-Quijada, D. and Arboledas, L. (2013). "The Clientelistic Nature of Television Policies in Democratic Spain," *Mass Communication & Society*, 16(2): 200–221.

Frattini, E. and Colías, Y. (1996). *Tiburones de la comunicación*. Madrid: Ediciones Pirámide.
Giordano, E. and Zeller, C. (1999). *Políticas de televisión*. Barcelona: Icaria.
Imbert, G. and Vidal Beneyto, J. (Eds.) (1986). *El País o la referencia dominante*. Barcelona: Mitre.
LA VANGUARDIA (2019). "Prisa obtiene un resultado negativo de 110 millones de euros hasta septiembre por provisiones," *La Vanguardia*, October 29.
Pérez Gómez, A. (2002). *El control de las concentraciones de medios de comunicación: Derecho español y comparado*. Madrid: Dykinson.
PRISA (1989). *Estatutos sociales Promotora de Informaciones, S.A.* Madrid: Prisa.
——— (2008). *Informe Anual*. Madrid: Prisa.
——— (2013). *Consolidated Annual Accounts*. Madrid: Prisa.
——— (2014). *Consolidated Annual Accounts*. Madrid: Prisa.
——— (2015). *Consolidated Annual Accounts*. Madrid: Prisa.
——— (2018). *Consolidated Annual Accounts*. Madrid: Prisa.
——— (2019). *Resultados 9M*. Madrid: Prisa.
Rosique, G. (2012). "Prisa: evolución, crisis y estrategias empresariales," in García Santamaría, J.V. (Ed.): *Los procesos de "financiarización" en los grupos de comunicación españoles y el caso Prisa-Liberty*. La Laguna: Cuadernos Artesanos de Latina.
Sanmartí, J.M. (2018). "La influencia de *El País*," in Guillamet, J. (Ed.): *La transición de la prensa: El comportamiento político de diarios y periodistas*. Valencia: Universitat de València, pp. 189–209.
Segovia, A.I. (2005). "Las contradicciones del sistema y los cambios legislativos en el ámbito comunicacional en España," in *V Congreso de ENLEPICC: "Sociedade do Conhecimento e Controle da Informação e da Comunicação"*. Salvador de Bahía, Brasil: Faculdade Social da Bahía.
Seoane, M.C. and Sueiro, S. (2004). *Una historia de El País y del Grupo Prisa*. Barcelona: Plaza & Janés.
Zarzalejos, A. (2019). "El regulador portugués de las 'telecos' bendice la venta de Media Capital (Prisa) a Cofina," *Vozpópuli*, November 11.

3 Economic Profile

From a financial and economic perspective, Grupo Prisa has certainly been the largest and most influential Spanish pure media conglomerate since the 1980s, after the launching of *El País*. After the newspaper consolidation, Prisa expanded intensively during the 1990s and the 2000s, trying to build a multimedia empire in the Spanish- and Portuguese-language markets, with some attempts at penetration into other markets too until its economic decline in the late 2000s.

During this 40-years process, Prisa has seen its economic profile radically transformed by its rise and crisis, its corporate strategy and expansion, its ownership mutation, its key linkages with politics, and its ties and dependencies with financial capital markets and actors. In this chapter we provide the historical data regarding corporate structure and financial and market share data for the company, as well as its corporate strategy and state of affairs at the end of the second decade of the twenty-first century.

Corporate Structure and Assets

As we established in Chapter 2, Prisa's corporate history can be divided into three stages according to the expansion of the firm (Almiron and Segovia, 2012):

- 1972–1983: Early years. Launch and consolidation of *El País*. The newspaper quickly became the most widely read and influential daily newspaper in the Spanish context of transition to democracy.
- 1984–2007: Cross-media expansion (anchored in the statute changes in 1984 described in Chapter 2). Prisa, which was already at that time the leading Spanish media group by revenues, intensively invested in the national and international markets until 2008. Directly or through its subsidiary, Sogecable, Prisa entered the television business at many levels: pay-TV, free-to-air television, and television and film production.

At the same time, the media group expanded its activities to magazines, printing, advertising, music, and book publishing (by taking over the activities of the Santillana group, a former publishing company owned by the Polanco family, Prisa's main shareholders at the time), while starting a very intensive process of acquisitions of international media assets. Some of the most relevant assets launched or acquired in this expansion period are listed in Table 3.1.

- 2008–Present: Crisis and divestment. After 2008, Prisa did not completely stop acquiring new assets.[1] However, from this date on, Prisa's trend of expansion was completely reversed, shifting to contraction and divestment.

Table 3.1 Grupo Prisa's Largest Media Investments, 1984–2007

Date - Market	Asset	Business
1984 - Spain	Acquisition of Cadena SER (100% by 1992)	National radio network
1989 - Spain	Acquisition of *Cinco Días* (100% by 1994)	Weekly business newspaper
1990 - Spain	Launch of Canal+ Becomes Cuatro in 2005	National terrestrial pay-TV
1990 - UK	Acquisition of *The Independent* (19% by 1992) Sold in 1998	Daily national newspaper
1992 - Portugal	Acquisition of *Público* (17%) Sold in 1997	Daily national newspaper
1992 - Spain	Takeover of Antena 3 Radio (main competitor of Prisa's radio network)	National radio network
1993 - Mexico	Acquisition of the publisher La Prensa (49%) Sold in 1996	Daily national newspaper
1996 - Spain	Acquisition of *As* (75%)	Second Spanish daily sports newspaper
1997 - Spain	Launch of Canal Satélite Digital	Satellite pay-TV
1999 - Colombia	Acquisition of Radio Caracol (19%)	National radio network
1999 - Spain	Launch of Gran Vía Musical (GVU) Sold to Universal in 2004	Music recording
2000 - Spain	Takeover of the activities of Santillana (part of Polanco's family assets)	Publishing

(*Continued*)

Table 3.1 (Continued)

Date - Market	Asset	Business
2000 - Bolivia	Acquisition of Grupo Garafulic's media assets (100% by 2003) Sold by 2010	Press, broadcasting
2000 - Spain	Launch of Localia Closed at the end of 2009	Local television network
2001 - Brazil	Acquisition of Editorial Moderna (100%)	Publishing
2001 - Mexico	Acquisition of Radiopolis (50%)	Radio broadcasting
2003 - Spain	Launch of Digital+ (after the merger Canal Satélite Digital-Vía Digital)	Satellite pay-TV
2004 - Argentina	Acquisition of Radio Continental and Radio Estéreo (100%)	National radio networks
2005 - Brazil	Acquisition of Editora Objetiva (75%)	Publishing
2005 - Spain	Launch of Cuatro Sold in 2010	National free-to-air TV
2005 - France	Acquisition of *Le Monde* (15.1%)	National daily newspaper
2005 - Portugal	Acquisition of Media Capital (94.4% by 2007)	Media conglomerate
2006 - Chile	Acquisition of IberoAmericana Radio Chile (100%)	National radio networks

Source: Compiled by the authors based on annual reports

Note: International investments in grey

The global economic and financial crisis starting in 2007 in the United States had a devastating effect in Spain,[2] and certainly played a role in Grupo Prisa's decline. However, as we argue later, the fragile financial situation of the company was its main problem. Hence, the global crisis made the profound financial crisis within the company no longer sustainable, and these financial problems spurred the company to make very substantial changes in its strategy and structure as well as in ownership, which will be further addressed in Chapter 4.

As far as corporate structure is concerned, between 2008 and 2011 Prisa sold and/or closed some of its most valuable assets, mostly in the broadcasting sector (see Table 3.2). Nevertheless, it also increased its interest in the Latin American education-publishing sector (as the purchase of the Colombian Grupo Norma illustrates), although leaving the book publishing

Table 3.2 Grupo Prisa Main Asset Divestments, 2008–2019

Date - Market	Asset	Business	Type of Divestment
January 2008 - Spain	Prisa Radio[1]	Radio broadcasting	8.14% sold to an investment fund (3i)[2]
December 2008 - Spain	Localia	Local TV network	Closed
2008–2010 - Bolivia	Grupo Garáfulic	Media conglomerate	100% sold to different investors
April 2009 - Spain	Crisol	Bookstores	Closed
September 2009 - Spain	Santillana	Main publishing subsidiary	25% sold to an investment fund (DLJ South American Partners, LLC)
December 2009 - Spain	Digital+	Satellite pay-TV	22% sold to Telefónica
			22% sold to Telecinco (Mediaset)
December 2009 - Spain	Cuatro	National free-to-air TV	100% sold to Telecinco (Mediaset)[3]
February 2011 - Portugal	Media Capital	Media conglomerate	10% sold to a Portuguese businessman[4]
June 2014 - Spain	Canal+	Satellite pay-TV	56% sold to Telefónica
July 2014 - Spain	Santillana Ediciones Generales	Publishing subsidiary of Santillana	100% sold to Penguin Random House
December 2017 - Spain	Dédalo Grupo Gráfico	Print subsidiary of Prisaprint S.L.	Closed
March 2018 - Peru	Prisa Radio Perú	Radio subsidiary	Closed
November 2018 - Costa Rica	GRL Costa Rica	Radio subsidiary, 50% Prisa Radio	50% sold to Multimedios
November 2018 - USA	Santillana USA Publishing Company	Publishing subsidiary of Santillana	Closed

Source: Compiled by the authors based on annual reports

Notes: International divestments in grey. (1) Formerly known as Unión Radio, this company was created in 2006 by Grupo Prisa (80%) and Grupo Godó (20%) to bring together their radio assets. (2) In 2019 Grupo Prisa repurchased this percentaje from 3i. That means that currently Prisa own the 80% of Prisa Radio. (3) The sale included some share swaps of Mediaset España, which Prisa sold to Mediaset years later (2014 and 2015). (4) Prisa bought back this 10% in 2013.

business (Prisa sold Santillana Ediciones Generales to Bertelsmann in 2014). Moreover, it is taking a step further in the international press sector, creating the national online edition of *As* (sport newspaper) in Arabic, a joint venture with the Qatari firm Dar Al Shark Group, with 49 per cent of the company owned by Diario As S.L., which will open the doors to 25 countries in North Africa and the Middle East.

In 2019, the corporate structure of Grupo Prisa was radically different from the corporate structure at its peak as a multimedia conglomerate. Table 3.3 provides a comparison with 2010 and the beginning of 2019.

By mid-2019, Prisa was divided into four business areas: education-publishing, radio, news (press), and media capital. The revenues originate 40 per cent from Spain and 45 per cent from the American continent.[3]

Education-Publishing (Santillana)

Grupo Santillana has been part of Grupo Prisa since 2000, and in 2018 it contributed almost half of Grupo Prisa's revenues (see Table 3.5), a total amount that exceeds 600 million euros. This includes the sale of textbooks and teaching-related services and materials. In 2019, Prisa held 75 per cent of shares of Grupo Santillana Educación Global, S.L. In 2009, 25 per cent of Santillana went to an investment fund (Victoria Capital Partners), but in February 2019 Prisa entered an agreement to buy back this 25 per cent for 312.5 million euros, which was completed in April 2019.

In June 2014, Grupo Santillana sold its Ediciones Generales to Penguin Random House (PRH) for 72 million euros, undermining the power of Santillana. The deal included publishing houses Alfaguara, Taurus, Suma de Letras, Aguilar, Objetiva, Altea, Fontanar, and Punto de Lectura and excluded the segment of activities of the children and youth division of Alfaguara, which is associated with Santillana's school business. Following this transaction, Santillana announced its intention to fully focus all its efforts in the area of education, which was undergoing a thorough digital and pedagogical transformation. Santillana's actions in Latin America include the expansion of the educational programs Sistema UNO (an integrated teaching service built around collaboration with school management, offering training and evaluation, bilingual education, and digitization of the educational system), Santillana Compartir, Farias Brito, and Educa (initiatives designed to introduce technology in schools in a less radical way than Sistema UNO). The Santillana Compartir system has spread through more than 2,000 schools and has more than one million users, with an outstanding international presence (in almost all countries of Latin America).

In the education business, Santillana holds a leading market position in virtually all countries where it operates. Regarding textbooks in 2018, it held a 19.9 per cent market share in Spain, and in foreign markets, it has high

Table 3.3 Grupo Prisa Main Media Assets, 2010 vs. 2019

Sector	Assets in 2010	Assets in 2019
Broadcasting	Pay-TV in Spain (Digital+) Free-to-air TV in Portugal (TVI) 17.34% of one of the leading commercial free-to-air TV networks in Spain (Telecinco, now Mediaset España) 32.95% of free-to-air TV in the US (V-me Media) Market leader in Portuguese TV and film production (Plural/NBP) One of the Spanish leaders in film productions (Sogecine)	Free-to-air TV in Portugal (TVI) Market leader in Portuguese TV and film production (Plural Entertainment)
Education (Textbooks)	Santillana (Spain) Moderna (Brazil) Santillana (Latin America)	Santillana (Spain) Moderna (Brazil) Santillana, Grupo Norma (Latin America)
Radio	Cadena SER (Spain) Media Capital (Portugal) Radio Caracol (Colombia) GRL Chile (Chile) 50% of Radiópolis (50% Televisa) (Mexico)	Cadena SER (Spain) Media Capital (Portugal) Radio Caracol (Colombia) GLR (Chile) 50% of Radiópolis (50% Televisa) (Mexico)
Press	Daily newspaper *El País* (Spain) 75% of the economics newspaper *Cinco Días* (Spain) Daily sports newspaper *As* (Spain) 15% of the daily newspaper *Le Monde* (France)	Daily newspaper *El País* (Spain) 75% of the economics newspaper *Cinco Días* (Spain) Daily sports newspaper *As* (Spain) Online sports newspaper in the Middle East and North Africa (AS, 49% Diario As S.L.) 20% of newspaper *Le Monde* (France)

Source: Compiled by the authors

shares in Argentina (39.6 per cent), Colombia (34.4 per cent), Chile (28.4 per cent), Brazil (21.9 per cent), and Mexico (16.6 per cent). The evolution of subscription models in the learning system represents more than a 20 per cent increase in revenues in comparison with 2011, with 1,375,000 students by the first quarter of 2019.

Radio

At present, Prisa Radio's shareholding structure is as follows: Prisa 80 per cent, and Grupo Godó 20 per cent. In February 2019 Prisa concluded the buy-back of the 8.14 per cent held by private equity fund 3i. In 2018, radio revenues reached 287.58 billion euros, of which 71 per cent came from Spain and 29 per cent from Latin America, mainly Colombia.

The main source of income for the radio business is advertising, with a small contribution from the organization and management of events and the provision of other ancillary services (through the subsidiary Planet Events). Prisa Radio is the largest radio group in Spain, reaching 22 million listeners and more than 40.5 million unique Internet users, according to their 2018 annual report. Prisa Radio has a direct presence in Argentina, Colombia, Costa Rica, Chile, Mexico, Panama, and Spain, and it has an indirect presence in other countries: the Dominican Republic, Ecuador, Guatemala, Nicaragua, and Paraguay. Prisa Radio is well positioned in the main Spanish-speaking markets and is the indisputable leader in Spain, Colombia (27 per cent market share), and Chile (40 per cent market share). The company has a twofold structure considering its business areas – radio and music – and the 12 countries where it operates.

In Spain, radio stands out for its competitive strength through its main stations: Cadena SER, 40 Principales, Cadena Dial, Los 40 Classic (formerly M80), Radiolé, and Los 40 Dance (formerly Máxima FM). In 2019, Cadena SER kept the leading position, with 4,148,000 listeners (a 37.6 per cent share in the general-interest radio market), while Los 40 and Cadena Dial were ranked number one and number two, respectively, in the musical radio segment, with audiences of 21.9 per cent and 16.3 per cent.

Furthermore, through Media Capital (see Table 3.1), Prisa holds 37 per cent of the radio market share in Portugal.

News (Press)

Prisa Noticias is the business unit focusing on the sale of newspapers and magazines, advertising, promotions, and print. It comprises leading brands: *El País, Cinco Días, As* (75 per cent), *El Huffington Post* (50 per cent), *Meristation, Rolling Stone, Guía del Ocio, Claves de la razón práctica,*

Buena Vida, *SModa*, *Retina*, *Icon*, and *Car*, in addition to other corporate magazines. It should be noted that the aggregate online readership according to the 2018 annual report is 125.9 million unique users.

In 2018, the press area experienced an 8 per cent decline in its revenues, and reached a little more than 200 million euros in revenue – 14 per cent of the total revenues, having been the most profitable business unit from the beginning of the century until 2005 (see Table 3.5). The digital transformation of the sector has provoked a decreasing circulation year over year: 68.3 million euros in 2018 (33 per cent of the revenues of the business unit) compared to 203,9 million euros in 2005; accompanied by the drop of offline advertising (-25 per cent). Nonetheless, this has been compensated for little by little by the increasing revenues in online advertising (28 per cent, 56.7 million euros in 2018).

The news business unit includes press sales, advertising, special promotions, and printing. The main commercial brands are *El País* and *As*, meaning that 90 per cent of the unit revenues come from these two newspapers (97 per cent of it originating in Spain). According to Oficina de Justificación de la Difusión (OJD), the bureau that audits circulation in Spain, Prisa's press market share in 2018 was 16.1 per cent.

El País, the leading general-interest newspaper in Spain, had a circulation of 137,552 in December 2018 (38 per cent market share) with an online worldwide audience of 83 million unique visitors (48 per cent international visitors). In spite of its leadership, *El País* has been losing readership constantly within the last decade (in 2007 the OJD certified that the newspaper had a circulation of 435,083 copies). Added to the gloomy picture was the internal crisis of the newspaper in 2012, associated with the layoff of 129 professionals out of a total payroll of 466 employees (almost 28 per cent of the total).[4]

In spite of this, it continued its international expansion of printing and distributing *El País* in various countries (Mexico, Argentina, Chile, Peru, Dominican Republic, Colombia, and the US) until last decade. Nevertheless, as of January 1, 2020, Grupo Prisa ended its print editions in Mexico and Argentina (the distribution in the other countries stopped in 2018), thus converting *El País* into a fully digital medium in the region. On the other hand, the company announced its intention to strengthen the editorial staff in Mexico City, which has about 20 journalists, hiring 14 new professionals – including editors and technological profiles – which will produce content focused on the Americas.

Regarding *As*, it is the second most popular sports newspaper in Spain (99,346 circulation in December 2018, with 45.8 million unique online visitors worldwide, comprising almost 52 per cent of international users). Interestingly enough, it is through this business that Prisa is expanding to new markets,[5] with a new online edition of *As* in Arabic.

Media Capital

In 2019 Prisa owned 94.69 per cent of Media Capital SGPS, S.A., the largest media group in Portugal[6] – and owner of TVI, Portugal's leading channel, with a daily average audience of 24 per cent of the overall audience share (27 per cent in prime time) – whose 2018 revenues were 181,809 million euros. However, its position in the broadcasting sector is a shadow of what it was (see Tables 3.3 and 3.5).

In addition to managing TVI, Media Capital manages five other pay-TV channels. TVI24, TVI Ficção, TVI Reality, TVI International, and África TVI, available in 22 countries and 40 audio-visual platforms. The Portuguese media group also holds Plural Entertainment, a prominent audio-visual production company (entertainment, fiction, documentaries, and animation) in the Portuguese market, with offices in Portugal, Brazil, and Spain.

The subsidiary Media Capital Radios is the most important radio group in Portugal, operating various networks: Rádio Comercial, M80 Rádio, Cidade FM, Smooth FM, and Vodafone FM. The radio market share of Rádio Comercial was 24.7 per cent in 2018, while M80 Rádio increased its market share to 8.5 per cent.

Brand Solutions

In addition to Prisa's four main business areas, it has Prisa Brand Solutions, the company division that sells advertising and includes La Factoría (The Factory) for the production of tailored content in both digital and traditional formats. It develops media on demand for other brands and creates content for third parties and specially branded content for Prisa Noticias (news). In 2018, this division generated associated revenues of around 10.9 million euros, 35 per cent more than in 2017.

Financial Data and Market Share

The financial health of Grupo Prisa directly correlates with the three main corporate stages of the conglomerate's development and the evolution of its shareholder structure, which will be further discussed in Chapter 4. From its beginning in 1976, the group rapidly achieved a break-even point, with pre-tax profits going from 0.25 million euros in 1977 to 5.7 million euros in 1984, when the cross-media expansion strategy began (Almiron, 2006). From that moment on, however, the numbers soar.

As can be seen in Table 3.4, it took Grupo Prisa almost a quarter of a century to surpass 1 billion euros in revenues (since it began operations in 1976), another six years to more than double that figure, and just a couple of years

Table 3.4 Grupo Prisa: Revenues, Net Results, and Financial Debt, 1999–2018 (Consolidated Financial Statements/Billions of Euros)

Year	Revenues	Net Income	Financial Debt
1999	959.000	86.000	98.000
2000	1.108	93.000	410.000
2001	1.197	78.000	567.000
2002	1.216	79.000	539.000
2003	1.251	62.000	621.000
2004	1.375	103.000	653.000
2005	1.426	153.000	603.000
2006	2.728	229.000	2.556
2007	3.696	262.000	3.296
2008	4.002	126.000	5.135
2009	3.209	65.000	4.985
2010	2.823	−35.000	3.705
2011	2.725	−395.000	3.703
2012	2.665	−338.000	3.231
2013	2.726	−1.029	3.508
2014	1.455	−2.310	2.873
2015	1.374	39.000	2.140
2016	1.358	50.000	1.858
2017	1.170	−76.000	1.765
2018	1.280	−237.000	1.351

Source: Compiled by the authors from annual reports and the Amadeus database

to go beyond 4 billion euros in revenues in 2008 – that was just before the global economic crisis reared its head in Prisa's financial accounts.

Financial debt was also marginal up to the cross-media expansion period and only achieved a relevant amount after 1999, when the conglomerate started to be listed in the stock exchange markets (in 1999 the broadcasting subsidiary, Sogecable, was launched, and in 2000 so was its parent company).[7] In 2008, the year that divestment began, financial debt achieved an unprecedented amount, more than 5 billion euros.

Until 2005, the largest part of Prisa's revenues came from the press segment and mainly from *El País*. The national daily newspaper accounted for 20 to 40 per cent of total group revenues. From 2006 on, the television segment business of the group (Sogecable), launched in 1990, was fully incorporated into Prisa's consolidated accounts (after Prisa took over a controlling stake in the company). That year, Grupo Prisa's consolidated financial statements almost doubled its total revenues and increased 50 per cent in its net results thanks to the Sogecable and Portuguese Media Capital incorporations. Therefore, that year's revenue distribution by segment was radically modified as well. From then on, the television broadcasting segment accounted for more than half of Prisa's revenues until the sale of all remaining Spanish television assets in 2014.

Additionally, as we can see in Table 3.5, after the incorporation of Sogecable's revenues into Prisa, the education segment became the second-ranked business segment by revenues, mainly because of the increasing sales in Latin America after some relevant acquisitions there (see Table 3.1). By contrast, in 2009, 65 per cent of Santillana's total education revenue came from Latin America and, in 2018, 18 per cent of total revenues were from Spain. In fact, these international revenues came from Brazil (29 per cent), Mexico (14 per cent), and Argentina (8 per cent). Because of the efficiency of this segment (low costs and low risks compared with the television broadcasting division), the Santillana subsidiary was considered Prisa's "crown jewel". Looking back to Table 3.2 we can see that the main assets sold by Grupo

Table 3.5 Grupo Prisa: Revenues From Segments, 1999–2018 (Percentages)

Fiscal Year	Press	Radio	Education[1]	Television Broadcasting[2]
1999	47.0	17.0	28.0	-
2000	48.0	17.0	28.0	-
2001	43.2	15.6	32.5	0.6
2002	33.2	15.2	28.5	1.1
2003	32.0	14.6	25.6	1.9
2004	38.2	15.0	25.7	3.0
2005	32.2	20.2	27.7	2.8
2006	14.8	12.5	17.2	44.6
2007	11.1	10.9	15.0	56.6
2008	8.6	9.8	15.0	53.1
2009	10.1	11.4	19.1	55.0
2010	15.0	14.0	23.0	49.0
2011	14.0	14.0	26.0	46.0
2012	12.0	13.0	28.0	47.0
2013	10.0	13.0	27.0	50.0
2014	17.9	21.0	49.3	12.4
2015	17.0	24.0	46.0	12.0
2016	17.0	23.0	46.0	13.0
2017	16.7	21.3	48.9	12.5
2018	15.9	22.5	46.9	14.2

Source: Compiled by the authors from public reports and presentations

Notes: Main segment by revenues in grey. (1) The education segment encompasses Prisa's publishing, educational, and training activities through its publishing arm, Santillana. (2) In the years 1999 and 2000, Grupo Prisa reported revenues from radio and television combined. Until 2006, revenues indicated from broadcasting came from local television. From 2006 until 2013, the Sogecable business was incorporated in Prisa's consolidated statements. From 2014 on, it includes only Media Capital.

Prisa in its divestment process from 2008 on were precisely in these two segments: broadcasting and education.

Prisa's education segment was also considered a precious asset in comparison to the television broadcasting subsidiary, Sogecable. The reason is that the latter raised Prisa's revenues but also was the reason for Prisa's big financial troubles. When Sogecable was incorporated into Prisa's financial statements, the company's financial debt multiplied by a factor of four, from 603 million euros to more than 2.5 billion euros in 2006. The figure even doubled the next couple of years and surpassed 5 billion euros by 2008. In fact, the main reason for its huge indebtedness was not Grupo Prisa's expensive market expansion (investing millions of euros in asset acquisitions), but rather Sogecable's history and the tactic used to face financial troubles (explained in the next section on corporate strategy).

Nevertheless, even though Grupo Prisa had by 2019 reduced some of its more relevant media investments, the company had been able to maintain its position as the leading firm in the Spanish market for almost 40 years with the exception of the broadcasting sector. Moreover, given the fundamental force of this segment in media and culture, we can maybe foresee its decline to a much less relevant position in the future. At this point, it is important to observe that a single man conducted this expansion strategy for two decades: former *El País* editor-in-chief and Prisa's CEO Juan Luis Cebrián, who in 2018 was forced to leave by the new shareholder structure.

Corporate Strategy

The expansion strategy of Grupo Prisa for four decades can mainly be explained in terms of typical capitalistic competition trends within an industry where television broadcasting became, since the market liberalization of the 1980s, the largest sector of the media in economic terms. Born as a newspaper publisher, like all traditional media groups in Spain, Grupo Prisa identified television broadcasting as the place where revenues could rocket, risks could be distributed, and economies of scale could be generated, mainly by sharing content through the different supports (radio and television with press and later with the Internet as well). The strong reputation of the *El País* brand was thought to be an added value for success. However, it is not clear whether the market expansion was devised as an economic expansion that was to take advantage of the prestige of *El País*, or whether it was mainly a political expansion designed to extend the newspaper's influence beyond the limits of the press[8] while also increasing revenues and profits along the way. Probably both reasons played a role. It's noteworthy to remember that Grupo Prisa did not go public until 2000, whereas the expansion strategy started well before that time, and even when the company was listed on the stock markets the Polanco family kept a controlling stake in ownership until the end of 2010 (up to 70 per cent). Therefore, risks of takeovers had not been a concern for Prisa's board of directors all those years. The desire for more influence and power, efforts to achieve corporate independence while getting ahead of competitors, and personal ambition probably best explain Prisa's expansion strategy up to 2008 before its eventual decline.

This strategy obviously did skyrocket revenues (and debt), but it did not distribute risks or increase the firm's efficiency. For Prisa, the main source of concern was actually its main area of expansion, the broadcasting sector, through its subsidiary Sogecable. In this respect, the roots of Sogecable's financial instability can be traced to the following issues, which are strongly tied to the Spanish corporate and political context of the time.

First, Sogecable had to confront a very costly strategy when building its satellite pay-TV platform, Canal Satélite Digital (CSD). At the time, a second platform led by Telefónica, called Vía Digital, was launched, in a context of politicization and extreme polarization of the Spanish media scenario during the first term of Partido Popular's government led by José María Aznar (1996–2000). The conservative cabinet of Prime Minister Aznar gave strong support to the building of this second satellite pay-TV platform as a means of counteracting the leadership of socialist party (PSOE) supporter Grupo Prisa. As a result, tough competition arose between both platforms for the key television broadcasting rights, mainly sports (football) and film rights (from major US film studios), which were considered crucial to gain subscribers. Eventually, Prisa's CSD won the content battle, but it came at an exorbitant cost increase. An auditor's report from 1997, the first year of operations for CSD, accounted for a syndicated 350-million-euro loan incurred by Sogecable for launching the platform. However, this was just a minimal portion of the company's launch expenses. For instance, an exclusive agreement with Time Warner for ten years accounted for 541 million euros, and Sogecable also signed agreements with the remaining major US film studios – Disney, Paramount, Sony Pictures, and Universal.

As far as Spanish premier league football is concerned, the battle for the broadcasting rights between CSD and Vía Digital – known as the first football war (1997) – turned the Spanish premier league into the most expensive league on the planet. The so-called League of Stars made the Spanish football clubs the richest in the world thanks to the skyrocketing increase in revenues from sports rights (Martínez Soler, 1998).

Mainly because of this, the platform supported by the Aznar government declined a few years later and Prisa's platform absorbed its competitor and created Digital+. That merger, which left Grupo Prisa as the sole player in the satellite pay-TV market in Spain, had a strong impact on the financial statements of the company. As reported by then CEO Juan Luis Cebrián (2008), Prisa took out a banking loan of 1 billion euros in 2002 to support this absorption.

The satellite pay-TV platform merger also meant the entrance of the Spanish telecom group Telefónica into Sogecable's ownership, reducing Prisa's stock holding to 16 per cent. According to Cebrián (2008), that was illogical in a successful business created by Prisa itself and was the reason why the company launched a partial takeover bid for 20 per cent of Sogecable in 2006 and a final takeover bid in 2007. That left 100 per cent of Sogecable shares in Prisa's hands, along with 2.9 billion euros of increased debt after entering into several syndicated loans and credit facilities with a group of banks to finance these operations.

Furthermore, to the Sogecable's managerial strategy we must add Sogecable's parent company's direct investments in broadcasting, which included the launch of costly failures in free-to-air TV (Localia and Cuatro). Prisa's ambition to penetrate all television broadcasting markets resulted in the closing of Localia, its local television network, after years of investment, mainly through acquisitions of local stations as well as the sale of Cuatro, its national free-to-air TV.[9] We can see the main reason for these failures in the context of strong competition among an increasing number of pay and free-to-air TV channels and the advertising investment crisis of 2008–2010, which will be analyzed later.

Last, we must mention another syndicated loan and credit facility for 450 million euros to finance Prisa's takeover bid for shares of Portuguese Media Capital and to meet the cost and expenses related to this acquisition, as Media Capital's main assets were broadcasting assets. Overall, the television broadcasting strategy of Grupo Prisa can be pointed out as the main cause of Prisa's financial distress.

Nevertheless, the origins causes of the financial debt don't portray a complete picture of why Grupo Prisa hasn't been able to build a media conglomerate as financially healthy as similar-sized European conglomerates such as Italian Mediaset, Finnish Sanoma, or German Axel Springer. We must look as well at the market and economic and political context.

The monopoly position of Prisa in the satellite television market is crucial to understand its attractiveness to shareholders and financial creditors since the beginning of the 2000s (a new market in Spain with high growth expectations where Prisa held the key content rights, as we have seen, for attracting subscribers). This good growth prospect, alongside Grupo Prisa's prestige in the press segment, coincided with a period of financial euphoria where raising money from financial markets was practically an effortless task. In reference to this fact, former Prisa CEO Cebrián (2008) stated in the extraordinary 2008 shareholders' general meeting:

> [Grupo Prisa has more than tripled its size since it went public] without any effort from its own funds, in the midst of a climate of abundant and cheap money, in which financial institutions were queuing in front of firms' headquarters inciting them to incur in more and more loans at interest rates that were practically negative.

However, the company's position and the financial global trend evolved into a radically different direction compared to the positive prospects made by financial analysts.

First, although the company was able to remain the sole player in the Spanish satellite pay-TV market, competition arose from new asymmetric digital subscriber line (ADSL) and cable pay-TV operators and myriad new free-to-air channels (due to the digital terrestrial television migration). Prisa's share of the total pay-TV market in 2014 (the last year with Sogecable consolidated into Prisa's annual results) in terms of revenues was still 60 per cent (CNMC, 2015), but this figure had been decreasing annually since 2004. Based on the number of subscribers, Prisa's share was 31.1 per cent in 2014.

Second, in 2014, Prisa's pay-TV revenue from Digital+ alone accounted for more than 40 per cent of its total income (revenues), a figure that clearly shows the dependence of the group's business on this segment. However, maintaining its leading position – and its key revenues – proved to be not as easy as expected. Although the company's plans were right as to what contents should be exploited to lead the market, being able to keep the television broadcasting rights turned out to be a totally different challenge. Film rights were renegotiable but Prisa lost key Spanish football league broadcast rights in 2007 when the so-called second football war started. The dispute erupted after Mediapro (Imagina Group) bilaterally signed contracts with the major Spanish football clubs and, as a result, left Digital+ without control over the source of half of its revenues (Nogales, 2010).

Third, financial expectations were even more difficult to meet. In fact, compared to most European markets, the low penetration of pay-TV in Spain is still considered a reason for high growth expectations in this market (33 per cent as of the end of 2016; DELOITTE, 2018), and therefore, a business that can still attract financial partners and investors. Additionally, pay-TV subscriptions are considered less sensitive to economic cycles (compared to free-to-air television and its dependence on advertising revenues). However, the economic downturn in Spain from 2008 to 2010 had an impact on Prisa's business in three aspects: (1) it affected pay-TV subscriptions: revenues from subscribers decreased as well as the number of subscribers, who moved to cheaper platforms with football broadcast rights or simply dropped pay-TV services; (2) the banking system refused to refinance Prisa's broadcasting debt; and (3) Prisa could not find additional new financial partners to support its business, which forced the company to share Digital+ ownership with industrial partners (Telefónica and Mediaset) and, eventually, to sell the whole firm.

After 2008, the financial crisis experienced by Grupo Prisa – along with global economic trends – forced a shift towards a redefinition of the corporate strategy. While the Spanish television business was abandoned, the company pretended to focus on consolidating its overseas presence and respond to the challenges posed by emerging information technologies.

On the one hand, as Cebrián stated in 2012 when he was still the company's CEO and chairman, Prisa was pleased with being redefined as a Latin American company rather than a Spanish company. This claim was supported by Latin America's share in the conglomerate's total revenues. Prisa's strategy in the Latin American and US Hispanic markets was also reflected by the fact that two prominent businessmen, Roberto Alcántara Rojas, president of Grupo Toluca (Mexico), and John Paton, CEO of Digital First Media (US), were appointed to serve on Prisa's board of directors in 2014.

On the other hand, the digital challenge posed by new media to all traditional media corporations had been a permanent struggle for Prisa. In 2013, the dismantling of Prisa's digital division put an end to an integrated digital strategy that included the creation of a platform that served as repository for the archive of all the company's media. The ambitious plan was dissolved for several reasons, including the lack of clear direction and the complexity of the company, but it was chiefly due to the growing lack of resources by Prisa in the context of economic global recession. The difficulty in monetizing digital content is a recurring one and Prisa is present in markets whose consumers are reluctant to pay for content. The permanent mantra of the company, as in the case of other major media conglomerates, has been a claim for undergoing a process of accelerated digital transformation across all businesses in the conglomerate.

Financialization and Survival

Prisa carried huge debt due to its aggressive expansion strategy, with heavy investments in multiplatform media assets across Spain and internationally (mainly in Latin America, Portugal, France, and the UK), and with a broadcasting subsidiary, Sogecable, which had an unsustainable level of leverage though it performed well in exchange markets until mid-2007. To escape from this highly leveraged scenario, the company took on more debt in 2007 while scrambling to come up with enough cash to help repayments of debt. The insanity of the strategy of multiplying debt in order to get rid of debt worsened when Prisa lost the main legal rights for Spanish football games, which caused a collapse of its stock. The sale of its television assets followed by the sale of portions of its flagship publishing house were the first steps taken to help the company survive and remain in compliance with creditors, mainly banking entities, for repayment of its debt. Prisa has always been among the top ten largest European media owners but also the most highly leveraged European pure news media company.

The financial rise and fall of Prisa followed a global trend among media corporations, and global corporations in general, which has been based on the US model of communication provision export around the globe and the global needs of top advertisers, whose industries have experienced the same level of concentration and increasingly transnational needs (McChesney, 2008). However, this logic – get very big very quickly in order to avoid being swallowed up – has not been without cost. Indeed, these corporations have made a huge financial and commercial effort, particularly for broadcasters but also print media groups. They eventually just reveal the same financialization pattern followed by all main industrial sectors in world economies. Overall, that is a clear indication of the degree to which all of them were dependent on the most volatile of all elements: financial leverage (i.e., borrowing money for corporate expansion). Nevertheless, a high level of unsecured debt was not the only cause for their weakness. A high degree of financialization of the strategy and goals of the whole media business is what an in-depth analysis of its links with the financial system strongly depicts (Almiron, 2010). Prisa was no exception, and it is the best example of the degree of financialization in European media companies – that is, the degree of dependence of financial leverage to go on doing business as usual.

The consequences of financialization in Prisa have been the same as those for the whole economy: despite its apparent strength and splendid growth during the 1990s up to the global (and Prisa's) crisis, Prisa suddenly exhibited high volatility. Jobs were cut, shutdowns were executed, assets were put up for sale, and insolvency threats started to emerge. Problems had existed even before the decline in advertising became truly evident. The global financial and economic crisis starting in 2007 in the United States exposed the extent to which global media conglomerates were built on top of sand castles.

At the end of the second decade of the twenty-first century the company was just trying to survive, but the fundamental challenges remained. What has made the news media an industry that requires large amounts of money has been the confluence of two main elements in the past decades: growth pressures due to concentration trends and high-tech transformation due to technological change. Both of these pressures remain. Investment in global expansion and expensive technologies dramatically increased the need for capital, chiefly as a result of the so-called digital convergence, which meant that the whole industry needed to redefine its business in the new digital era. What was initially sold as a way to radically reduce costs for traditional media (bits for paper) turned out to be, in most cases, a complex and expensive transformation. Furthermore, the fact that the technology allows for the production of all kinds of media content far more easily has brought about a large number of small- and medium-size competitors online that, at least for news content, have become insurmountable competition.

By way of conclusion for Grupo Prisa's financial and economic evolution, some contextual variables can explain the financial volatility of such a top European media conglomerate, as well as give lessons for the future.

First, we argue that the huge financial support received by Grupo Prisa throughout its history is due to a combination of the following factors: the success, prestige, and political influence of *El País*; the original deluded belief that there was no true competition to Sogecable in the television broadcasting segment; and the periods of financial euphoria of the last two decades alongside the high expectations and promises of growth and wealth placed on the information and communication sector. To these must be added the affinities and linkages of Grupo Prisa with politics, which will be addressed in Chapter 4.

Second, we maintain that the financial crisis of Grupo Prisa was not produced by the global 2008–2010 financial turmoil but by structural factors linked to its historical strategy of growth. This strategy had been able to move forward, in spite of its irrationality in terms of financial balance, because of the support given by the banking system for the reasons we will see in next chapter. The global financial crisis was the banking system's excuse for stopping its support of Prisa's leverage, but other reasons should be considered as well: Prisa's television broadcasting business was not as secure as analysts promised, while the gradual chilling of the traditional good relations between Prisa and the socialist governments (PSOE) in the last years may also have played a role. The former would reflect the well-known paradox that in competitive capitalism financial investors prefer to invest mainly in businesses without real competition. Coincidence or not, Prisa's leverage ceased to be supported by the banking system when its pay-TV and broadcasting rights businesses didn't look like a monopoly anymore.

Third, we assert that there has been an increasing financialization of Grupo Prisa throughout its history, mainly since it went public in 2000. Financialization here means that financially driven or even speculative actors increasingly penetrated within ownership and management, and financial dependence increased through the rocketing leverage. Thus, Prisa's values and premises

44 Economic Profile

have been progressively overwhelmed by its financial troubles, which co-opted the goals and attention of top executives. In this sense, the company's financialization led, paradoxically, to a severe financial crisis within Prisa, which in turn led to a very severe corporate restructuring addressed solely by financial efficiency goals. This restructuring had an extremely negative impact on the level of independence of Prisa and it threatens to reduce even more the levels of professionalism, content quality, and pluralism in the Spanish media system.

Finally, we can extract some general lessons from the Grupo Prisa case study. First, multimedia expansion strategies can make risks skyrocket and efficiency diminish at very high levels for medium-sized companies. Second, such difficulties can be overcome when companies have strong financial support, but this is always tied to other independent and unpredictable variables (global economic trends, media sector prospects, influence and political support of media firms, etc.). Third, internationalization forces manifest in radically different ways among national sectors (while Spanish telecommunications and banking companies have very successfully penetrated Latin American markets, this hasn't been the case for Spanish media groups) and thus are hard to foresee. Lastly, we cannot measure the fall of media companies solely through economics. Grupo Prisa was, by money-making parameters, the largest news-media company in Spain. However, if we take out of its income the revenues provided by its education business (Santillana), Prisa has been outscored by the Spanish private television broadcasters Mediaset España and Atresmedia[10]. However, during its growth and crisis processes, Prisa has undermined its most emblematic hallmark: credibility and corporate independence.

Notes

1. For instance, after 2009 it acquired several stakes of shares of V-me Media, a public television network in the United States, broadcasting only in Spanish (most of them then sold in 2013); in 2011 it acquired *Meristation*, a Spanish magazine devoted to online videogames; in 2016 it acquired the education publisher Grupo Norma, operating in Colombia, Argentina, Chile, Guatemala, Mexico, Peru, and Puerto Rico; and in 2017 Prisa Brand Solutions obtained Latam Digital Ventures (focused on advertising sales in digital media in Latin American and US markets).
2. According to the National Statistics Institute (INE, Spain), the gross domestic product (GDP) of Spain decreased by 3.7% in 2009 and 3% in 2012, making these the worst two years of the new century for the Spanish economy.
3. The information detailed in this section has been extracted from the company public records (web, annual reports, consolidated accounts, executive summaries, and presentations from the years recorded).
4. See Chapter 4 for more data about the number of employees in the group today.

5. First in the United States through First Colombia S.A.S. in July 2015, Diario AS US, Inc. in October, and Noticias As México, S.A. de C.V. in November (all of them 100% Diario AS, S.L.).
6. As reported in Chapter 2, at the end of September 2019 Grupo Prisa announced the sale of Media Capital to the Portuguese firm Cofina. However the transaction was not completed since Cofina backed out of the agreement in March 2020 (REUTERS, 2020).
7. It is relevant to note that Prisa's shares even reached the exclusive IBEX 35, the main stock market index of the Madrid Stock Exchange, two times: from November 2000 to July 2003 and from January 2004 to January 2007 (BOLSA DE MADRID, 2019).
8. According to Daniel Hallin and Paolo Mancini (2004), elites in Mediterranean countries mainly consume the paid press.
9. We have no sources to evaluate Localia launch and closing costs, while Cuatro shares were exchanged for an ownership interest of 17.34% of the share capital of the new Telecinco resulting from the integration of Cuatro within it (sold in 2015, as already noted; see Table 3.2, note 3).
10. In 2018 Atresmedia and Mediaset España declared close to 1 billion euros in revenues, when that of Prisa Noticias, Prisa Radio, and Media Capital was less than 700 million euros.

Bibliography

Albornoz, L.A. (2007). *Periodismo Digital: Los grandes diarios en la Red*. Buenos Aires: La Crujía Ediciones.
Almiron, N. (2006). *Poder financiero y poder mediático: banca y grupos de comunicación. Los casos del SCH y PRISA (1976–2004)*. Doctoral dissertation. Barcelona: Autonomous University of Barcelona.
———. (2010). *Journalism in Crisis: Corporate Media and Financialization*. Creskill, NJ: Hampton Press.
Almiron, N. and Segovia, A.I. (2012). "Financialization, Economic Crisis, and Corporate Strategies in Top Media Companies: The Case of Grupo Prisa," *International Journal of Communication*, 6: 2894–2917.
BOLSA DE MADRID (2019). *Historical Constituents IBEX 35*. Madrid: Madrid Stock Exchange.
Cebrián, J.L. (2008). *Prisa's Chief Executive Officer Statement. Extraordinary Shareholders*. General Meeting, Madrid, Spain, December 5.
CNMC (National Commission for Markets and Competition, Spain) (2015). *Informe Económico Sectorial de las Telecomunicaciones y el Audiovisual 2015*. Barcelona: CNMC.
DELOITTE (2018). *Informe Conecta 2018*. Madrid: Deloitte España.
Doyle, G. (2002). *Media Ownership*. London: Sage Publications.
Hallin, D. and Mancini, P. (2004). *Comparing Media Systems*. Cambridge: Cambridge University Press.
Martínez Soler, J.A. (1998). *Jaque a Polanco*. Madrid: Temas de Hoy.
McChesney, R.W. (2008). *The Political Economy of Media: Enduring Issues, Emerging Dilemmas*. New York: Monthly Review Press.

Nogales, A.I. (2010). "La llegada de Liberty Acquisition Holding al accionariado de Prisa y sus consecuencias," In Zallo, R. and Badillo, A. (Eds.): *Mercado y políticas de cultura y comunicación en el mercado global*. Proceedings of the 3rd National Conference of ULEPICC España, Salamanca University.

PRISA (2018). *Annual Report*. Madrid: Prisa.

REUTERS (2020). "Portugal's Cofina pulls plug on TVI acquisition as market turmoil scuppers capital hike". March 11.

4 Political Profile

This chapter addresses the shareholding structure of Grupo Prisa, which has been substantially altered since the process of debt refinancing the company experienced during the 2000s. In this context, what we can consider as the founding family, that of Jesús Polanco's, has lost power to new shareholders from the finance and business sectors. These changes are reflected in the composition of the board of directors in 2019. In addition, this chapter provides data on the company's labour force, as the number of employees dropped considerably in the period from 2010 to 2019.

Finally, the relationships developed by Prisa with the Spanish state, which includes the Crown, top economic and financial powers, and the democratic governments that followed since the early 1980s, as well as some Latin American governments, are outlined. They reflect both the harmony with different state establishments and the clashes with some governments.

Ownership

This section introduces the transformation of the ownership of Grupo Prisa from a family-owned company into an institutional investor-owned company.[1] We interpret it as a financialization process, following work carried out by critical economists (pioneered by Epstein, 2005).

Promotora de Informaciones S.A. (Prisa), the parent company of Grupo Prisa, was incorporated in the city of Madrid on January 18, 1972, by a group of five individual investors, and that group quickly increased its number to 400 in 1973 and to more than 1,000 in 1976. Thus, Prisa's first ownership was dispersed among dozens of small shareholders who shared a common trait: they all belonged to the Spanish upper class. Among them, there were relevant figures from the Spanish cultural, political, and economic spheres. It is interesting to note that all of them were characterized as having centrist or conservative political views, which are very "moderate" views quite different from the tenets held by *El País* in 1976 (Seoane and Sueiro, 2004: 30).

In the following years, however, one of the least politically and culturally significant shareholders, Jesús Polanco (1929–2007), was able to progressively increase his stockholding to become the dominant shareholder by 1984 – the year that Grupo Prisa changed its statutes (see Chapter 3) – with 40 per cent of Prisa's shares. Polanco was the owner of a publishing education house, Editorial Santillana, later incorporated into Prisa, and he was able to maintain control of Prisa without interruption until his death in 2007. In fact, between 1984 and 2010, no other shareholder (except the Polanco family) would hold more than 10 per cent of Prisa's shares.

As Table 4.1 shows, going public in 2000 didn't stop Prisa from being a family owned company, since the Polanco family kept almost 70 per cent of the stocks under their control for almost ten years after the initial public offering. However, the attention of Prisa's management was increasingly shifted from corporate goals to financial goals due to the growing leverage. In fact, the degree of financial leverage pushed the Polanco family to accept the Liberty-Prisa business combination at the end of 2010, jointly planned by Prisa CEO Juan Luis Cebrián and several international investors.

Liberty Acquisitions Holdings was a special-purpose acquisition company, that is, a collective investment scheme that allows public stock market investors to invest in private equity-type transactions, particularly leveraged buyouts. The combination of the Liberty and Prisa businesses meant that all Liberty funds were incorporated into Prisa (up to 650 million euros), as well as all the individual financial investors that made up Liberty which, in turn, dissolved as a company.

According to the company, "the Liberty transaction was intended to return leverage to sustainable levels" (PRISA, 2010), but it also meant an increase in the financialization of Prisa, that is, a radical strengthening of the links and dependencies of the company on financial actors and goals.

Grupo Prisa's administration had been, however, linked to financial capital well before the Liberty operation. Several members of Prisa's board have always had direct links – current or former – with financial entities and, since the company went public, dozens of Spanish and international equity funds bought Prisa's shares, some acquiring up to 5 per cent of stock, as was the case with both the US custodian banks State Street Bank and Trust and Artisan Partners. Sogecable itself, the audio-visual branch, was actually launched and consolidated with the support of several Spanish banking entities: Banco Bilbao Vizcaya Argentaria (BBVA), Banca March group, Bankinter, and Caja Madrid. These entities remained in Sogecable's ownership until almost 2006. Additionally, Sogecable was listed in Spanish stock markets from 1999 to 2006.

However, from 2010 on the financialization of the ownership grew up to the point that the funding family stock was reduced to below 10 per cent by

Table 4.1 Grupo Prisa's Ownership, 1972–2018

Month/Year	Shareholders
January 1972	Five shareholders: José Ortega Spottorno (publisher), Carlos Mendo (journalist), Darío Valcárcel (journalist from *ABC* newspaper), Juan José de Carlos (lawyer), and Ramón Jordán de Urríes (aristocrat)
May 1972	45 shareholders (Jesús Polanco already among them)
June 1972	337 shareholders
May 1977	1,096 shareholders
1980	Jesús Polanco becomes the main stockholder with 10% of shares
1983	Jesús Polanco takes control of Prisa with 40% of shares
1992	Signing of the shareholders agreement among the Polanco family and several other shareholders close to them to pool their shares under the control of Jesús Polanco, who then holds 72.5% of Prisa's shares
2000	Public offering of 25% of Prisa; after going public, the Polanco family still controls 68% of shares
2010	Liberty Acquisitions incorporates into Prisa Polanco family (Jesús Polanco died in 2007) keeps 30% of Prisa's shares; the remaining 70% goes public and is mostly held by institutional investors
2018	Financial debt forces several shareholding structuring during the period 2010–2018 that leaves the funding family with 15.4% of the stock and one single investment fund (Amber Capital) with 26% of the shares

Source: Compiled by the authors from Seoane and Sueiro (2004) and Prisa's annual reports

50 Political Profile

Table 4.2 Grupo Prisa's Ownership, October 2019

Shareholders	% Voting Shares
Joseph Oughourlian (through Amber Capital UK LLP controlling Amber Active Investors Limited, Amber Global Opportunities Limited, and Oviedo Holdings SARL)	29.8
Telefónica S.A.	9.443
HSBC Holdings PLC	9.108
Polanco's family and partners (Rucandio)	7.611
Sheikh Qatari Khalid Thani Abdullah Al Thani	5.142
Mexican businessman Roberto Alcántara Rojas (through GHO Networks SA de CV)	5.018
Mexican businessman Carlos Slim (through Inversora Carso)	4.305
Banco Santander S.A.	4.145
Mexican businessman Carlos Fernández González	4.027
Melqart Opportunities Master Fund Ltd (UK investment manager)	3.285
Others	18.116

Source: CNMV, October 2019

2019 (see Table 4.2). Financial institutions held the majority of the stock, with one single individual investor not linked to the founding family holding up to almost 30 per cent (Lebanese businessman Joseph Oughourlian, mostly through Amber Capital) – it was on the brink of a compulsory takeover bid.

It should be noted that, due to the capital increase process undergone by Grupo Prisa, in recent years investors of all types have been coming and going. Such is the case, for example, of the Israeli fund Adar Capital Partners LTD, owned by the Argentine-Israeli financier Zev Marynberg, who entered Prisa's shareholding in February 2019, came to own 7,292 per cent of the shares, and then completely withdrew in March of the same year (Rodríguez, 2019; Pérez Navarro, 2019).

Political Links

Since its birth, Prisa has established relations with all of the political and economic elites, including the Spanish monarchy and the top corporate businesses. Although considered an ideologically "progressive" media group during its first two decades of existence, Prisa was calculatedly created to occupy a niche market in the Spanish transition towards democracy. In this context, ideology was used as a marketing asset, but within clear limits determined by business interests.

It is worth recalling the context in which Prisa was born. After four decades of a fascist regime, the death of Franco's dictatorship did not bring about the restoration of the democratic republic that was deposed by the military, but a transitional pact promoted by the regime's elites. That is, the so-called transition to democracy was piloted by the elite of the Francoist regime (Gallego, 2008). Thus, when democracy was restored in Spain in 1976, there was no purge of Franco's supporters either at the state level – including senior civil servants, police chiefs, the judiciary system, or the military system – or in the economic and media sphere. The Spain that emerged after 1976 inherited the structural corruption of the old regime as well as its ideological aversion to multiculturalism, multinationalism, and multilingualism.

At the same time, and for this very reason, the transition to democracy did not mean the end of the institutional para-police and extreme-right violence, as suggested in the myth of an exemplary, peaceful Spanish transition to democracy (Baby, 2017). This transitional period was a turbulent time when fear and violence reigned. In this context, the military elites forced into the Spanish 1978 Constitution three principles that became the three taboos of the newborn democracy. These were the indissoluble unity of the Spanish nation, the unquestionability of the monarchic system, and the indisputable right of the military to influence and intervene in Spanish politics if any of the former two were at risk. In this way, the legal underpinnings of the new democratic constituent courts emanated from the Francoist court system. It was through the Law of Succession that Franco appointed Juan Carlos de Borbón as his successor in 1966, and it was the Francoist courts that proclaimed him king in 1975. This is why the current Spanish monarchy is considered the successor of Franco by republicans in Spain.

Not surprisingly, the elites piloting the Spanish transition to democracy also opted for silence. As Alfons Aragoneses (2017) remembers, there were no trials nor even condemnations of the dictatorship and no references either to the anti-Francoist opposition or the victims of Francoism. This contrasts sharply with the dissolution of fascist regimes in other European countries during the twentieth century. Interestingly, all mainstream Spanish media joined this silence on the problematic roots of the new restored democracy. Prisa's media was no exception.

The roots of Grupo Prisa were actually totally entangled with this reality. Prisa's founder, Jesús Polanco, was a successful, Catholic, Falangist entrepreneur in Franco's regime (Cabrera, 2015), while Juan Luis Cebrián, the editor in chief of *El País* during the first decade, was hired by Polanco because of his perfect pedigree for the Francoist leaders attempting to lead the political transition: "He was a child of the regime, of the Salamanca neighborhood, of well-off bourgeois families" (Seoane and Sueiro, 2004: 53). At that time Cebrián was not only a journalist with "strong Francoist connections, who had worked for the newspapers *Pueblo* and *Informaciones*, as well as for the news broadcasts of Televisión Española", but he was also a young professional with "good connections with the opposition [to Francoism], acquired fundamentally through his studies in Philosophy at the Complutense University and the Catholic magazine *Cuadernos para el Diálogo*" (Sanmartí, 2018: 190). Cebrián's father, a lifelong Falangist, had occupied prominent positions in the media system under fascist control,[2] and his son would become the most powerful Prisa executive for over four decades.

Throughout Prisa's existence up to 2018, when Cebrián was finally removed from all relevant positions within the company, the relationship between Prisa and the different democratic administrations went through different stages.

Right after the restoration of democracy, the good relationships and concordance between Grupo Prisa and the Felipe González (PSOE) governments (1982–1996) is well known. While the socialist administration supported Prisa's business, the media group provided favourable news coverage for government actions. After González lost power, several of PSOE's leaders – Jorge Semprún (former Minister of Culture of Spain during 1988–1991, in a Felipe González government, although he never became a member of the PSOE), Carlos Solchaga (former Minister of Industry during the first mandate of Felipe González, and later Minister of Economy of Spain) and Miguel Ángel Fernandez Ordoñez (economist and civil servant, who was a member of several PSOE governments) – landed in Prisa as either managers or advisors.

The situation during the conservative José María Aznar government (1996–2004), from the Partido Popular (PP), meant a U-turn. The Aznar administration organized an offensive against Prisa's business expansion projects through the instrumentation of the Spanish telecommunications company Telefónica, and managed to prosecute Prisa's leading officers (a case that vanished into thin air), raising the concerns of intellectuals, newspaper directors, and professionals in Europe and America. However, in spite of the strong confrontation in the journalistic, legal, and economic fields, Prisa maintained privileged relations with renowned PP leaders, including Rodrigo Rato (former Managing Director of the International Monetary Fund during 2004–2007, currently in prison), Alberto Ruiz Gallardón (former Minister of Justice of Spain during 2011–2014), Pío Cabanillas Alonso (former Minister Spokesman for the government of José María Aznar during 2000–2002), and Rodolfo Martín Villa (he held several relevant political positions during Franco's dictatorship; during the Transition, he was part of the government team of Adolfo Suárez; and in democracy he was among the ranks of UCD first and PP later). Pío Cabanillas Alonso and Rodolfo Martín Villa even took management positions in Prisa.

Days before the end of the Aznar government, *El País* was involved in a strange episode that revealed a degree of ingenuity of the Spanish press in its relations with political power. On the morning of March 11, 2004 (popularly known as 11-M), a local cell of Al Qaeda made ten backpack bombs explode simultaneously in four trains on the outskirts of Madrid. The bloodiest terrorist attack in the history of Western Europe (192 people dead and over 1,800 injured) was committed three days before Spain held its general elections. The question of the cause of 11-M – and particularly, in an electoral context, of its immediate political consequences – was soon raised. If the separatist organization ETA (an acronym for *Euskadi Ta Askatasuna*; Basque Country and Freedom) was the cause of the virulent attack, the PP would be favoured in its electoral chances (the Aznar administration had fought ETA effectively and had wielded its policy against ETA terrorism as an electoral weapon against the PSOE and the Basque and Catalan nationalist parties). Conversely, if 11-M was the work of a radical Islamic group, this could be interpreted as a response to the Spanish participation, advocated by the PP, in the invasion of Iraq led by the United States in 2003.[3]

Hours after the attack, and while the leading newspapers were preparing their special editions, phone calls were made from the seat of government to various media outlets in an effort to hold ETA responsible for the massacre. In an unprecedented event, president Aznar telephoned the directors of major newspapers in Madrid and Barcelona to insist that ETA was responsible for the terrorist attacks, ruling out other possible avenues of investigation. One of these calls was answered by then director of *El País* Jesús Ceberio, who decided to change the headline on the cover that would have opened the special edition, replacing the original headline, "Matanza terrorista en Madrid" ("Terrorist Slaughter in Madrid"), with "Matanza de ETA en Madrid" ("ETA Slaughter in Madrid"), without even mentioning the source of information. This was a regrettable decision, which resulted from a scheme of lies and information manipulation orchestrated by the PP leaders in office, one which subsequently garnered Prisa's newspaper severe criticism.

The historic error of *El País*, also committed by almost all mainstream newspapers in Spain (including *ABC*, *El Periódico de Catalunya*, *La Razón*, and *La Vanguardia*), was partially offset by the outstanding performance of Cadena SER in the days following the terrorist massacre. Prisa's main radio network was one of the media outlets that set the intensive news pace of those days with a series of exclusive scoops on how the reporting developed, giving special coverage to protest rallies that took place outside the headquarters of the PP in Madrid and other Spanish cities after the hypothesis of Islamic responsibility gained strength. On the Sunday after 11-M, the Spanish people, already aware of the scheme that had been orchestrated by the government, gave their votes to PSOE against the results of opinion polls that had been conducted before 11-M, which were placing the PP on the verge of an absolute majority.[4] Through these elections, and this bizarre media episode, socialist José Luis Rodríguez Zapatero arrived in office.

The relations between Grupo Prisa and the Rodríguez Zapatero administration (2004–2011), though not characterized by the tough confrontation of the previous stage, were far from harmonious like the Prisa and PSOE relationship in the past. The momentum of Grupo Mediapro,[5] a supporter of the Rodríguez Zapatero government that acquired football match broadcasting rights, challenged Prisa's monopoly as the three-decades-long linchpin of alleged progressivism. The subsequent legal decree authorizing pay-digital terrestrial television, and enabling Mediapro to premiere the channel Gol TV, aroused a very hostile reaction in Prisa. Prisa CEO Cebrián made a call for action in one article, to "each and every self-respecting democrat", against such "governmental abuse" (Cebrián, 2009). Prisa's overtly anti-Rodríguez Zapatero stance caught the attention of the international press; it even received coverage in *The New York Times* (Carvajal, 2009).

During Rodríguez Zapatero's government, an event would take place that was unprecedented in democratic times: in March 2007, the PP announced that it would stop attending "all the calls for interviews, talks and programmes of Grupo PRISA and other companies controlled" by its president, Jesús Polanco, as long as he did not "publicly and unequivocally rectify" the statements he made denouncing the difficulties faced by the company's media in carrying out their journalistic work in a political environment marked by tension and confrontation. Polanco, likewise, had denounced the Spanish right for currently maintaining positions "that distance it considerably from this profile of moderate conservatism" (EL PAÍS, 2007).

The history of the relationship between Prisa and the conservative Mariano Rajoy (PP) administration (2011–2018) represented, however, a complete turn in Prisa's allegiances. During this stage, a clear turn to the right emerged, mainly expressed by the news coverage of its most influential media: *El País* and Cadena SER. During this period, the critiques of the conservative government smoothed, and an aggressive attack against the new politically leftist group Podemos emerged.[6] Also, a meaningfully and explicit defence of the Spanish Crown was undertaken while a patriotic nationalist stance was adopted in front of the Catalan independentist challenge (Almiron, 2018).

This process of ideological rapprochement to conservative or even far-right positions, represented by right wing political parties PP and Ciudadanos,[7] persisted during the new administration of socialist Pedro Sánchez, once PSOE was back to office after winning a non-confidence motion in the Parliament in June 2018.

Overall, the extent to which the media group has distanced itself from its former support for the socialist party is blatantly shown in the editorials of *El País* and by some board directors of the period praising the populist right party Ciudadanos (Landaluce, 2018).

Another front of analysis is the relationship between Prisa and Latin American governments (of note, former Mexican President Ernesto Zedillo served on the Prisa board from 2010 to 2017). In its relations with Latin American governments, the company's ideological stance seems to be closely intertwined with its business interests. On the one hand, the company reacted against a Latin American government when the findings of research performed by left wing political group Izquierda Unida (IU) on the role of the United States and Spain in the unsuccessful coup d'état against Venezuelan President Hugo Chávez in 2002 revealed "the shameful role of Grupo Prisa and, particularly, of newspaper *El País* in support of the coup". IU's parliamentary advisor, José Manuel Fernández (2013), said:

> *El País* has acted as the figurehead of the Polanco empire and its subordinates in Venezuela, where Chávez did not want to give Polanco any rights on TV and textbook sales. It is no secret that publishing house Santillana . . . has a network deployed in Latin America, where it has juicy textbook and school materials distribution contracts with the governments of several Ibero-American states. The publishing company has been granted numerous soft loans, and has won bids with the Development Promotion program of the Economy Ministry and the Spanish Agency for International Development Cooperation.[8]

Later, in 2014, the company acted this time in favour of a Latin American government. On the occasion of the Mexican president's visit to Spain in 2014, Mexican magazine *Proceso* claimed that newspaper *El País* "had virtually become the lobbyist of Enrique Peña Nieto during his official visit", giving him an opportunity to "promote his reforms and announce his National Infrastructure Plan to members of the Spanish large capitals". The role played by Prisa was directly related to its business in Latin America, it argued, noting, "[t]he model of promotion undertaken by *El País* is no news" and adding that it had already been tried with the governments of Colombia, Panama, Brazil, Chile, Peru, and Mexico, in Felipe Calderón's term of office (Gutiérrez, 2014).

Also, Prisa has shown to be extremely active at an institutional level in Spain and abroad. For instance, in 2014, through *El País*, the group hosted a wide range of discussion forums and debates with top-level government officials and business leaders from different Latin American countries (including events like Investing in Colombia; Mexico: Reforms for Growth; Investing in Puerto Rico; Investing in Chile; and Development, Innovation and Regional Integration). Further, in partnership with the Fundación Santillana, high-level events were held in the cities of Bogotá, Brasilia, and São Paulo with a focus on education (PRISA, 2015).

Board of Directors and Interlockings

Prisa's board of directors has experienced a radical transformation over the years in parallel with the radical changes undergone by its ownership. From the first five-member board of directors at its inception in 1972, including Prisa funders holding 100 per cent of the ownership, Prisa's board has expanded to reflect the complex network of ties the company has developed over time through ownership and interlockings.

Before the Liberty operation, in 2011, Prisa's board was known for including a majority of members of the Polanco family or directors linked to it. This situation continued even after the company went public in 2000 (the audio-visual subsidiary Sogecable went public the year before) because of the ownership control that the Polanco family held for many years after going public. Up to this moment, the directors at Prisa's board kept mostly corporate ties, not financial ties (though the Sogecable subsidiary had many financial ties on its board). A study conducted on the 2004 board of directors, for instance, showed board interlockings of Prisa and Sogecable with top companies from the key economic sectors in Spain like Roche Farma, Universal Music Group, Altadis, Media Planning Group, Gas Natural, Logista, Vivendi, Havas, Viscofan, Fomento de Construcciones y contratas, Cementos Portland, Abengoa, Telefónica, Lafarge Asland, Unión Fenosa, and Sacyr Vallehermoso, among others (Almiron, 2006).

However, this board's profile changed with the Liberty operation. The business combination with Liberty presented an opportunity for Prisa to gain access to the international capital market through its issuance of shares in the United States. This takeover also meant, nevertheless, a complete transformation of the ownership and of the composition of the board of directors of the Spanish media company. After the operation, Prisa's board incorporated seven new members, reducing the number of administrators close to the Polanco family to seven plus Prisa's CEO (Juan Luis Cebrián). As many as three of the new members were directly linked to equities funds (Nicholas Berggruen, Martin E. Franklin, and Emmanuel Roman) while some star characters from business and politics made their entrance into Prisa's board as well, including Alain Minc (French businessman), Ernesto Zedillo (former president of Mexico), Juan Arena (former Bankinter chairman), and Harry Sloan (former Metro-Goldwin-Mayer CEO).

More than ever before, Prisa's board of directors reflected the company's diversified network of corporate, financial, and business ties after 2011. In March 2019, Prisa's board included, besides the CEO (Manuel Mirat) and the Polanco stock (Timon), two directors representing the investment fund Amber Capital, two directors representing Qatari investment funds, three directors linked to Mexican assets (including a business leader of passenger transport in Mexico, Roberto Alcántara), three directors linked to Spanish

Table 4.3 Grupo Prisa's Board of Directors in October 2019 and Interlocking Directorates

Member	First and Last Appointments	Appointed By	Examples of Board Interlockings
Manuel Mirat (CEO)	June 2017	Executive Position	—
Javier Monzón (Non-executive Chairman)	November 2017	Independent Director	Openbank/Banco Santander (Spain) 4iq (US) Former Chairman of Indra (1993–2015)
Joseph Oughourlian (Non-executive Vice Chairman)	December 2015	Amber Active Investors	—
Manuel Polanco (vocal)	April 2001 April 2016	Timon (Polanco's family company)	—
Roberto Alcántara (vocal)	February 2014 June 2019	Consorcio Transportista Ocher	Grupo Toluca VivaAerobus IAMSA (Inversionistas en Autotransportes Mexicanos, S.A. de CV – Investors in Mexican Transport) Grupo Herradura Occidente (Mexico)
Khalid Thani Abdullah Al Thani (vocal)	December 2015 April 2016	Qatar Funds	Qatar International Islamic Bank Ezdan Holding Group (Qatar) Dar Al Sharq Printing Publishing & Distribution Co. Dar Al Arab Publishing & Distribution Co.
María Teresa Ballester Fornés	July 2019	Independent	Repsol, S.A. Afera Investments, S.L.
Fernando Martínez Albacete	March 2018	Amber Capital UK	—
Dominique D'Hinnin	May 2016 June 2019	Independent	EUTELSAT, EDENRED (France) Louis Delhaize (Belgium)

(Continued)

Table 4.3 Continued

Member	First and Last Appointments	Appointed By	Examples of Board Interlockings
Javier de Jaime Guijarro	November 2017 November 2017	Independent	CVC Capital Partners (Luxembourg) Theater Directorship Service Alpha Rioja Bidco Shareholdings Clara Visión
Sonia Dulá	November 2017 November 2017	Independent	CVC Investment Advisory Services Bank of America Merrill Lynch (US) Acciona Hemisphere Media
Javier Gómez-Navarro Navarrete	November 2017 November 2017	Independent	Viajes Marsans Técnicas reunidas (Spain)
Beatrice de Clermont-Tonerre (vocal)	June 2019 June 2019	Independent	CEVA Logistics Klepierre, a European specialist in shopping centres (Paris listed company) Until June 2018 the vice chairwoman of *Hurriyet*, the leading Turkish newspaper

Source: Compiled by the authors based on Grupo Prisa's board of directors and board committees, October 2019 (see: www.prisa.com/en/info/board-of-directors-and-board-committees-1)

assets (including the board of one of the Banco Santander subsidiaries), and another linked to French interests (including European Telecommunications Satellite Organization-EUTELSAT).

The interlockings of Prisa's board are only a reflection of its ownership shift towards an increasing presence of corporate, business, and financial interests. Grupo Prisa has been the largest and most influential purely media conglomerate in Spain since the 1980s and thus has occupied a very prominent position from which to make or protect business – even if with an ultimately poor financial investment return. Meanwhile, this financialization and corporatization of its board has pushed for an even further reduction of the watchdog role of the media group. As a result, Prisa has become fully embedded in the very masculine ethos of power and money – with female directors being an exception (Table 4.3).

Labour

Grupo Prisa has increased its number of employees as it has been undergoing a process of business growth (diversification of activities through acquisitions and mergers) and internationalization (expansion into Latin America). If we look at the data for Prisa since the beginning of this century (see Figure 4.1), it is possible to see a growth in its workforce that reached its apex in 2008 when the company registered 15,195 employees. The year 2008 will be recorded in world history because it was the beginning of an international economic crisis that severely affected Spain. For Grupo Prisa, 2008 is also a unique year, as the company simultaneously reached records of 4.002 billion euros in revenues and 5.135 billion euros in financial debt.

The refinancing and payment of the gigantic debt accumulated by Prisa in a short interval of time led the company's managers to take action in order to significantly reduce the number of workers. Over the past years, there has been significant downsizing in Spain through the so-called employment regulation orders (*expedientes de regulación de empleo*, EREs) – a regulated process enabling companies in Spain to apply mass layoffs and cuts in compensations as well as voluntary retirements. This downsizing process has left thousands of professionals jobless.

In January 2011, Prisa announced a restructuring and operational efficiency plan that would include 2,500 layoffs throughout the world. The plan would be rolled out through the first quarter of 2012. "The headcount reduction . . . is due to restructuring and personnel downsizing efforts, and to the non-substitution of employees at all our companies, mainly in Spain", explained the company (Toledo, 2014). Between 2008 and 2015, Grupo Prisa's headcount was reduced by 6,552 jobs, which represents a decrease of more than 40 per cent of its total workforce. The bulk of the reduction was in Spain, and it impacted all professional categories.

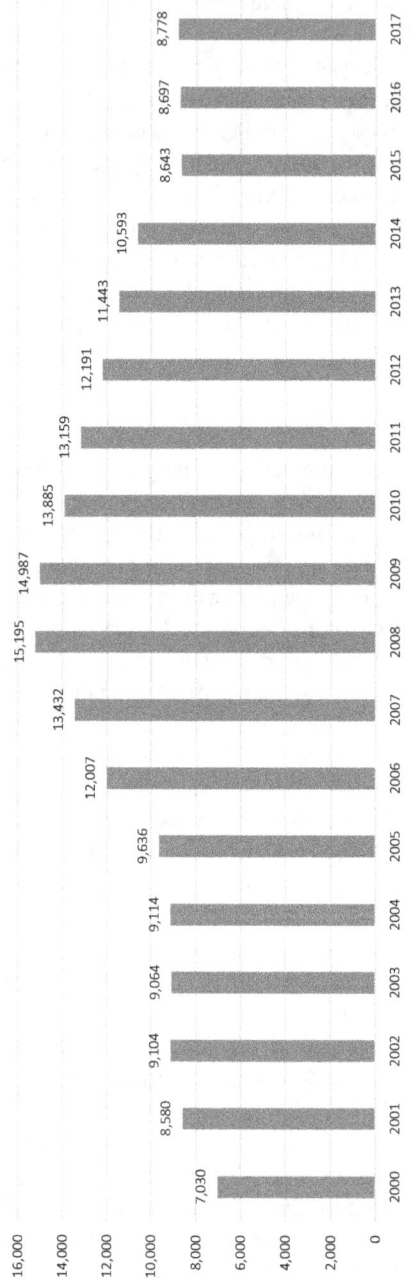

Figure 4.1 Grupo Prisa: Number of Employees, 2000–2017

Source: Compiled by the authors based on the following Prisa reports: Annual Report 2004, 2005, 2007, 2008, 2010, 2011, 2012, and 2013; Sustainability Report 2014; and Social Responsibility and Sustainability Report 2015, 2016, 2017, and 2018.

Note: For the report on workforce indicators, criteria were changed in fiscal year 2017. The average number of employees was reported until 2016, and from 2017 onwards, the figure reported is the number of active employees on December 31.

The main justification for the constant dismissals of workers has been the necessary restructuring of the company's business units to guarantee their own economic viability. And the direct consequence of these layoffs has been the increased workload among many of Prisa's employees. In addition, workers had to face wage reductions or freezes in order to avoid collective dismissals. For example, Prisa Radio's collective bargaining agreement valid for the 2019–2020 biennium states that from January 1, 2019, the salary reduction suffered by workers from 2014. That was the year in which the workforce accepted salary cuts (between 3 per cent and 7 per cent for workers who were paid 20,000 euros or more per year) to avoid an ERE that would affect 300 people, after 260 workers had been laid off in 2011 (Cano, 2019).

The ERE that affected the publisher of the newspaper *El País* in 2012 was particularly traumatic and controversial; it even had news coverage in foreign newspapers such as *Frankfurter Allgemeine Zeitung* (Ingendaay, 2012), *The New York Times* (Minder and Pafnner, 2012), and *Libération* (Musseau, 2012). The dismissal of 129 workers, including some of Spain's best journalists, "was much more than a labour crisis" (REALITY NEWS-MONGOLIA, 2013: 43). As the collective involved in the satirical magazine *Mongolia* argued, it was a drastic measure to save 14 million euros while the company's CEO, Juan Luis Cebrián, had just pocketed 12 million in 2011 as a member of the labour council – including bonuses. This collective reflected that this action

> was presented without a single semester of losses in three decades.... In one decade the daily earned more than eight hundred million euros, and in view of the first projection of future losses it shed a third of its workforce....
>
> None of this would have been possible without Mariano Rajoy's labour reform. *El País* was heavily criticised for taking advantage with the ERE of a rule that it criticised in theory, but this is a misunderstanding. The Prisa leadership knew what it was up to and in the editorial piece evaluating it ("El ajuste va en serio", February 11, 2012) the writer applauded that "reaching three quarters of decline in sales will allow the employment adjustment mechanism to be implemented".
>
> (idem, 2013: 45)

Based on the current location of the direct jobs generated by the company's activities, it can be seen that Prisa is a transatlantic conglomerate based in the Iberian Peninsula rather than a global giant or "a global group", as defined in its 2018 Social Responsibility and Sustainability Report. At the beginning of 2018, Prisa generated 8,778 direct jobs, nearly 48 per cent of which correspond to the Spanish and Portuguese markets (3,087 and 1,110 workers, respectively). The remaining 52 per cent – 4,581 workers – were distributed in 21 countries on the American continent (103 employees in the United

States included). Four markets accounted for 68 per cent of the force used by Grupo Prisa outside the Iberian Peninsula: Colombia with 1,263 employees, Brazil with 810, Mexico with 561, and Argentina with 477.

In addition, it should not be forgotten that the company's various activities generate indirect employment through the hiring of a wide range of freelance collaborators and professional services. Spain, Chile, and Brazil are, in this order, the countries with the highest number of external collaborators.

Grupo Prisa's principles include "special attention to compliance with equal opportunities between men and women in access to employment, career advancement, training, job stability and equal pay" (PRISA, 2018: 86). Despite this, the truth is that unlike other companies that prepare and publicize diversity and inclusion plans with the goal of promoting employment in groups historically marginalized from media management (such as women, persons with a disability, immigrant groups, LGBTQ persons or, in the case of countries with a colonial past, indigenous communities), Prisa has not established explicit initiatives regarding the composition of the labour forces that make up its business units in the respective operating markets.

In any case, the data provided by Prisa reveal that towards the end of the second decade of the twenty-first century (1) the majority of the workforce was made up of men, (2) the vast majority of employed people had a permanent contract, and (3) the majority of senior managers of foreign affiliates were of local origin.

In this regard, it should be pointed out, first of all, that although the fact that 46 per cent of the labour force hired by Prisa – 4,019 employees – is made up of women gives the impression of gender parity, the reality is that women are a minority in three important labour categories defined by the company: executives, middle management, and qualified technical personnel. The greatest difference is in top manager positions, with 34 percentage points in favour of male employees.

With regard to the type of contract, 93 per cent of Prisa's total workforce has a permanent contract (indefinite employment contracts or representatives of fixed trade, RRCF), while the remaining 7 per cent has a temporary contract (temporary contracts, temporary or representatives of temporary trade, RTC). This is particularly important for a company whose parent company is located in a country with a historically high unemployment rate, even in good economic times, and which is witnessing the recovery of the percentage of people employed on the basis of an increasing number of part-time and temporary contracts. On the other hand, labour markets in most of the Latin American countries where Prisa operates are characterized by high rates of informality and job insecurity, and by wage and access gaps between women and men regarding positions of responsibility.

Finally, the data show that Prisa encourages the recruitment and promotion of locally sourced managers. Thus, in most of the Group's markets there

Political Profile 63

is a high percentage of top managers (both first and second level) from the country in which the activity is carried out. In 15 of the 19 markets in which Prisa operates, the proportion of local senior executives to the total number of senior executives in each country is 75 per cent or more.

Corporate Social Responsibility

Since the beginning of the present century, Spanish companies have integrated in its business planning and management the notion of corporate social responsibility (CSR), viewing it as a key driver of public relations to improve the reputation and social legitimacy of a company, while conveying a certain corporate identity.[9] Media groups, including Prisa, have not avoided this trend and have included in their various programs a number of voluntary commitments to economically, socially, and environmentally responsible behavior.

However, it should be noted that there is an open debate in Spain about whether CSR is helping to transform the internal culture of the companies or whether, on the contrary, "everything has been a gigantic hoax to make social marketing and simply try to improve corporate reputation" (Jáuregui, 2014). Protecting reputation has become crucial for large Spanish companies, making Spain, overnight, the fourth greatest publisher of annual CSR reports. However, CSR legislation is so lax that, of the 3.1 million companies in the Spanish market, just 0.008 per cent must comply with some kind of requirement. And, in any case, it is enough for companies to apply the "comply or explain" principle; that is, to declare whether they meet a certain objective or proposed goal, or to explain why they do not comply (Fernández, 2015).

In this context, Grupo Prisa has gone from being one of the most important Spanish transnational companies that did not assume any type of public commitment in CSR matters, to developing a whole coordinated strategy of policies and actions with respect to its multiple stakeholders: employees, customers, suppliers, contractors, shareholders, public administrations, citizens, and society in general. With the explicit aim of creating value for stakeholders, leading sustainability in the sectors of communication and education in Spanish and Portuguese, this change is evident in the very name the company gives to the report that presents its annual performance: having previously been titled the "annual report", from 2015 on it was called the "social responsibility and sustainability report".

In its race to join the new wave of CSR, in December 2008 Prisa joined the United Nations Global Compact, a non-binding UN pact to encourage businesses worldwide to adopt sustainable and socially responsible policies and to report on their implementation.[10] Prisa's adoption of the ten principles of the Global Compact implies taking on a series of commitments in the areas of human rights, labour relations, preservation of the environment, and the fight against corruption that are made public through the so-called progress report. In 2010 and 2011, the Spanish Network of the United Nations Global Compact congratulated Prisa for its reports, given the quality of the information, the organization of the document, and the initiatives carried out by the company and its different business units to integrate CSR into the company's management.

However, it should be noted that the only obligation of the organizations that adhere to the Global Compact is to keep the progress report by which they are considered to be accountable to society up to date. As Pedro Ramiro and Alejandro Pulido (2009: 12) state:

> The Global Compact is characterized by the notable lack of definition of its contents – barely ten generic principles on human rights, the environment, labor rights and corruption – and the absence of any minimum supervision mechanism: the information that is communicated is voluntary, unilateral and without any kind of controls; but it does provide the UN endorsement to define itself as a responsible Company.

In 2015, one year in advance and on a voluntary basis, Prisa prepared its report in accordance with the then new version of the world's most widely used non-financial reporting standard, the Global Reporting Initiative (GRI, G4 guide).[11] Prisa's Social Responsibility and Sustainability Report 2015 highlights the "responsible management of communication" carried out by this transnational conglomerate in the following way (PRISA, 2015):

> PRISA's Corporate Communication and Marketing has a proactive approach focused on the permanent improvement of the Group's reputation. The strategic keys are based on integral communication, permanent research and analysis, positioning, segmentation and 3.0 communication to correctly manage corporate identity, internal communication, external relations and social responsibility.
>
> Aware of the importance of coordination for a group of companies present in 22 countries, and with a broad portfolio of products and services, it is essential to have an adequate communication network. At PRISA we have two permanent forums for communication and internal dialogue. Firstly, a weekly Communication Committee, which brings together the communication directors of the different business units, together with the head of Human Resources, Analysts and Investors and Transformation, to correctly direct internal and external communication activities at all levels. Secondly, the Social Responsibility Observatory, which every month takes the pulse of the progress of the action plans and the trends for their constant monitoring.

In addition, in 2015 Prisa's board of directors approved its Code of Ethics, one of the pillars of the company's corporate governance. The following year, the company revised and updated both this document and its materiality matrix in order to incorporate the new UN Sustainable Development Goals (SDGs) for the period 2015–2030 into its 2017 report.

Of note, the so-called commitment assumed in terms of CSR coexists with speculative trading in the stock market (Soteras, 2014) or complaints of labour law violations. These considerations lead us to believe that so-called CSR is more cosmetic than a genuine initiative to infuse business culture with socially desirable values.

Through various promotion and sponsorship agreements over the past few years, the company's outlets have become loudspeakers for human rights and development campaigns promoted by many recognized national and international organizations: United Nations Children's Fund (UNICEF), World Wide Fund for Nature (WWF), Oxfam Intermón, Fundación de Ayuda contra la Drogadicción (FAD, Spain), Ayuda en Acción (Spain), Spanish Red Cross, Manos Unidas (Spanish Catholic Church), Médecins sans Frontières, Save the Children, Office of the United Nations High Commissioner for Refugees (UNHCR), Food and Agriculture Organization of the United Nations (FAO), and United Nations Educational, Scientific and Cultural Organization (UNESCO).

Within its CSR strategy, Prisa has used several social marketing tactics. In this respect, a fundamental element of Prisa is its flagship publication, *El País*, by which the company organizes numerous discussion forums with the highest government and business authorities in Latin America and with important opinion leaders. The 40 years of uninterrupted democracy in Spain have been propitious for Prisa in that they have coincided with the lifespan of *El País*. Thus, the newspaper took advantage of this occasion to celebrate the Spain 40-40 Forum during 2017 and 2018, a series of meetings held in Madrid, Brussels, and London. With the participation of personalities from the social, cultural, economic, and political spheres in Spain and abroad, these meetings served, on the one hand, to reflect on the past, present, and future of Spain in Europe and the world. On the other hand, they strengthened the association of democracy, the welfare state, and *El País* as "a witness to and participant in" a process in which Spain "reach[ed] its highest ever levels of development and prosperity".[12]

In the field of education, Prisa and Fundación Santillana – through their headquarters in Madrid (created in 1979), Bogotá (1989), Buenos Aires (2004), São Paulo (2008), Lima (2015), and Santiago de Chile (2016) – develop programs of activity in the education and culture landscapes in collaboration with numerous institutions and with the ministries of education and culture of the respective countries. In the area of university education, the company has various agreements with Spanish and Latin American universities. With the Universidad Autónoma de Madrid (UAM) it develops the activities of the School of Journalism UAM-El País and the Master of Governance and Human Rights of the Jesús de Polanco Chair of Ibero-American Studies. It also collaborates with the Universidad Internacional Menéndez Pelayo (UIMP, Spain), the Instituto Tecnológico de Monterrey (TEC, Mexico), and the Mario Vargas Llosa Chair, an initiative of the Fundación Biblioteca Virtual Miguel de Cervantes with universities, companies, and cultural and educational institutions from Spain, Mexico, Peru, Colombia, the United States, France, and Sweden. In addition, Prisa, together with companies such as Indra, Telefónica, Grupo Santander, and IBM, is one of the sponsors of the CYD Foundation (Knowledge and Development), which promotes excellence in Spanish universities through reports and rankings.

A remarkable and consolidated practice of Grupo Prisa is the awarding of prizes to outstanding figures from the worlds of journalism, arts, and sports. Currently, Prisa awards several prizes, with their respective categories, each year:

- Premios Ondas: awards given annually to audio-visual professionals (radio, television, radio advertising, and music). They have been awarded by Radio Barcelona, a station of Cadena SER, since 1954. They are the first radio and television awards instituted in Spain, for which they enjoy great prestige.
- Premios Ortega y Gasset: created in 1984 by *El País* in memory of the Spanish thinker and journalist José Ortega y Gasset, to reward the best works published in Spanish-language media around the world. The jury for these awards is made up of important personalities from the communication sector and from economic, social, and cultural life.
- Premios Dial. awards given since 1996 by the Spanish music radio station Cadena Dial to the most successful Spanish-language artists and groups each year.
- LOS40 Music Awards (formerly Premios 40 Principales): created in 2006 on the occasion of the 40th anniversary of the music radio station Los 40 worldwide. The main prizes are awarded by popular vote among its listeners in Spain and eight Latin American countries. Since 2012, listeners in America have their own Premios 40 Principales América and have disassociated themselves from the Spanish awards.
- Premios AS del Deporte: annual awards granted by *As* (sport newspaper) since 2007. The prizes are awarded by popular vote by the readers of this sports newspaper. For example, in December 2017, the King and Queen of Spain presided over the 50th anniversary gala of *As*, in which the best Spanish athletes, such as the tennis player Rafael Nadal, the

swimmer Mireia Belmonte, and the British athlete Sebastian Coe were awarded prizes.
- Premios Cinco Días a la Innovación Empresarial: organized by the business-focused newspaper *Cinco Días* and sponsored by Caixa Bank and Repsol to reward the most innovative business initiative linked to the university in the field of new technologies and CSR.
- Premios Radiolé: in 2015 the radio station Radiolé (a musical radio-formula that broadcasts a selection of Spanish music, mainly *copla, rumba, flamenco,* and *sevillanas*) began these awards every year, which recognize the careers of artists.
- WDM Radio Awards: an award ceremony created in 2017 by Los 40 under their World Dance Music brand, billed as "the first radio awards to electronic music". It is meant to be a global event, promoted by the 12 Los 40 stations in Spain and Latin America.

The system of institutional prizes created by Prisa over the decades places this private-commercial conglomerate in the role of prescribing and defining the media-cultural canon in Spain and in several Spanish-speaking Latin American countries. Curiously, these awards, which contribute to oiling the internal and external political relations of Grupo Prisa and to disciplining its workforce, include workers and collaborators from the different units of the conglomerate, positioning Prisa as "judge and party".

Overall, Prisa is an excellent example of the balance between hegemony and ideology, as Vincent Mosco put it: "Hegemony is . . . more powerful than ideology because it is not simply imposed by class power, but constituted organically out of the dynamic geometries of power embedded in social relations throughout society" (Mosco, 1996: 242).

Notes

1. Institutional investors are organizations that trade large amounts of securities. Therefore, they are always large organizations linked with financial goals (investment banks, mutual funds, brokerages, insurance companies, pension funds, etc.).
2. Vicente Cebrián was a high-ranking member of the press during Franco's regime and director of the newspaper *Arriba* (1935–1936), the communication organ of Falange Española (FE), a political party of Falangist ideology (a fascist-inspired political doctrine) founded in 1933 by José Antonio Primo de Rivera.
3. Spain participated in the decision to invade Iraq at the Azores summit on March 16, 2003, where Spanish Prime Minister José María Aznar met with UK Prime Minister Tony Blair and US President George W. Bush and were hosted by Prime Minister of Portugal José Manuel Durão Barroso. The invasion was the first stage of the Iraq war and was decided before having made use of all available peaceful avenues of negotiation. A total of 2,600 Spanish soldiers were sent to Iraq between June 2003 and May 2004.

4. For more detailed information, see the works of Rekalde et al. (2004) and Artal (2004).
5. Grupo Mediapro is a Spanish audio-visual group from Barcelona founded in 1994 whose sole administrator is the businessman Jaume Roures. It produces content for cinema and television, manages sports rights and audio-visual services, and performs other associated services. Mediapro has 58 offices in 36 countries and owns 4.23% of the shares of Atresmedia Corporación.
6. Podemos is a left wing political party in Spain founded in January 2014 in the aftermath of the 15-M Movement protests against inequality and corruption.
7. Ciudadanos is a right wing political party in Spain founded in March 2006 with opposition to Catalan nationalism as its main core topic.
8. Translated by the authors.
9. The Green Paper presented by the Commission of the European Communities (CEC) in July 2001 sets out the most accepted definition of CSR: "a concept whereby companies integrate social and environmental concerns in their business operations and in their interaction with their stakeholders on a voluntary basis" (CEC, 2001: 6).
10. On July 26, 2000, the Global Compact was officially adopted at the UN headquarters in New York, with the participation of 44 transnational corporations – such as BP, Nike, Shell, and Novartis, among others – and some NGOs. The UN Global Compact is now the world's largest sustainable development initiative involving more than 13,000 companies from 160 countries.
11. The 2018 report corresponding to the activities carried out by Prisa in the 23 countries in which it operates was prepared in accordance with the criteria established in the new GRI Sustainability Reporting Standards and in accordance with the Global Compact principles.
12. In this regard, see the website that El País dedicates to the Spain 40-40 Forum: www.eventoselpais.com/cicloespana/en/.

Bibliography

Almiron, N. (2006). *Poder financiero y poder mediático: banca y grupos de comunicación. Los casos del SCH y PRISA (1976–2004)*. Doctoral dissertation. Barcelona: Autonomus University of Barcelona.

———. (2018). "'Go and Get'em!' Authoritarianism, Elitism and Media in the Catalan Crisis," *The Political Economy of Communication*, 6(2), 39–73.

Aragoneses, A. (2017). "Legal Silences and the Remembrance of Francoism in Spanish Law," In Belavusau, U. and Gliszczyńska-Grabias, A. (Eds.): *Law and Memory: Addressing Historical Injustice by Law*. Cambridge: Cambridge University Press, pp. 175–194.

Artal, R.M. (2004). *11-M – 14 – M. Onda expansiva*. Madrid: Ediciones Espejo de Tinta.

Baby, S. (2017). *Le mythe de la transition pacifique: violence et politique en Espagne (1975–1982)*. Madrid: Casa de Velázquez.

Cabrera, M. (2015). *Jesús de Polanco*. Barcelona: Galaxia Gutenberg.

Cano, F. (2019). "Cadena Ser acaba con los recortes y sube salarios por primera vez desde 2014," *El Español*, February 5.

Carvajal, D. (2009). "El País in Rare Break with Socialist Leader," *The New York Times*, September 13.

Cebrián, J.L. (2009). "Un Desatino," *El País*, August 21.
CEC (Commission of the European Communities) (2001). *Green Paper: Promoting a European Framework for Corporate Social Responsibility*. Brussels, 18.7.2001COM(2001) 366 final.
CNMV (National Securities Market Commission, Spain) (2019). *Promotora de Informaciones S.A. Notification of Voting Rights and Financial Instruments*, October.
EL PAÍS (2007). "El PP anuncia un boicot a todos los medios del grupo PRISA," *El País*, March 23.
Epstein, G.A. (Ed.). (2005). *Financialization and the World Economy*. Northampton, MA: Edward Elgar.
Fernández, J.M. (2013). "La colaboración de España y EE.UU. en el golpe de estado en Venezuela de 2002," *sinpermiso.info*, March 10. http://old.sinpermiso.info/articulos/ficheros/golpe.pdf.
Fernández, M. (2015). "La empresa se juega su papel social," *El País*, February 6.
Gallego, F. (2008). *El mito de la Transición: la crisis del Franquismo y los orígenes de la democracia (1973–1977)*. Barcelona: Editorial Crítica.
Gutiérrez, A. (2014). "El diario *El País*, cabildero de Peña Nieto," *Proceso*, June 13.
Ingendaay, P. (2012). "Kasino-Kapitalisten fressen Journalisten," *Frankfurter Allgemeine Zeitung*, October 22.
Jáuregui, R. (2014). "Responsabilidad Social Corporativa: ¿una experiencia frustrada?" *El País*, November 13.
Landaluce, E. (2018). "Alain Minc: 'Rivera inventó antes que Macron el populismo 'mainstream'," *El Mundo*, May 12.
Minder, R. and Pfanner, E. (2012). "Spain's Troubles Catch Up with a Storied Newspaper," *The New York Times*, October 23.
Mosco, V. (1996). *The Political Economy of Communication*. London: Sage Publications.
Musseau, F. (2012). "*El País*, gracias patron!" *Libération*, October 23.
Pérez Navarro, C. (2019). "El fondo de inversión israelí Adar Capital aumenta su presencia en PRISA mientras Amber se consolida como principal accionista," *Insurgente.org*, April 5.
PRISA (2004–2013). *Annual Report*. Madrid: PRISA.
———. (2010). *Investor Presentation*, September 17. Retrieved from www.sec.gov/Archives/edgar/data/1159513/000095012310087220/g24673exv99w1.htm.
———. (2014). *Sustainability Report*. Madrid: PRISA.
———. (2015–2018). *Social Responsibility and Sustainability Report*. Madrid: PRISA.
Ramiro, P. and Pulido, A. (2009). *Las multinacionales españolas y el negocio de la responsabilidad. Análisis de la Responsabilidad Social Corporativa de las empresas transnacionales en Colombia*. Bogota: Observatorio de Multinacionales en América Latina (OMAL).
REALITY NEWS-MONGOLIA (2013). *Papel mojado: La crisis de la prensa y el fracaso de los periódicos en España*. Barcelona: Debate.
Rekalde, A., Alba Rico, S., Pereira, R., Giacopuzzi, G. and Salutregi, J. (2004). *11-M: tres días que engañaron al mundo*. Tafalla: Editorial Txalaparta.
Rodríguez, C. (2019). "Amber se queda al borde de la opa por Prisa tras la salida del fondo israelí Adar," *LaInformacion.com*, March 25.

Sanmartí, J.M. (2018). "La influencia de *El País*," in Guillamet, J. (Ed.): *La transición de la prensa. El comportamiento político de diarios y periodistas*. Valencia: Universitat de Valéncia, pp. 189–209.

Seoane, M.C. and Sueiro, S. (2004). *Una historia de El País y del Grupo Prisa*. Barcelona: Plaza & Janés.

Soteras, J. (2014). "Cebrián especuló con acciones de Prisa meses antes de lanzar la OPA que estranguló al grupo en 2007," *InfoLibre*, June 2.

Toledo, D. (2014). "Prisa da por cerrada la crisis tras enseñar la puerta a 3.750 trabajadores en un lustro," *El Confidencial*, May 2.

5 Cultural Profile

Symbolic Universe and Ideology

In his work *The Media and Modernity*, John B. Thompson explains that power "is the ability to act in pursuit of one's aims and interests, the ability to intervene in the course of events and to affect their outcome" (Thompson, 1995: 13). He also points out the possibility of distinguishing between four main forms of power: economic, political, coercive, and symbolic. These are, in any case, different types of power that "commonly overlap in complex shifting ways" (Thompson, 1995: 14).

In this chapter, we are particularly interested in the notion of cultural or symbolic power, in order to reflect on the way(s) in which the media conglomerate Grupo Prisa has intervened in the political and cultural field both in the past and the present. Thompson explains that symbolic power – a notion he takes from Pierre Bourdieu – "stems from the activity of producing, transmitting and receiving meaningful symbolic forms". Since symbolic activity is "a fundamental feature of social life", its power lies precisely in the capacity of symbolic actions to intervene in the course of events. Since symbolic actions

> may give rise to reactions, may lead other to act or respond in certain ways, to pursue one course of action rather than another, to believe or disbelieve, to affirm their support for a state of affairs or to rise up in collective revolt.
>
> (Thompson, 1995: 16–17)

In the ensemble of actors who take part in the daily battle to give meaning and value to the events we take part in or do not take part in but which influence our lives, the media – with their orientation "towards the large-scale production and generalized diffusion of symbolic forms in space and time" (Thompson, 1995: 17) – alongside educational institutions have a prominent place.

72 Cultural Profile

Since the last quarter of the twentieth century, Grupo Prisa has been a conglomerate which, through its companies and brands, participates very actively in the Spanish fields of information, culture, and education. Deftly, and mainly through newspaper and magazine publishers, electronic media, and publishers of educational textbooks and works of fiction, Prisa has exercised (and continues to exercise) its symbolic power in Spain and in its natural areas of influence, which include primarily Europe and Latin America.

In the field of information, as mentioned earlier, it is worth highlighting two general media outlets that have a prominent place in the daily life of contemporary Spain and that, to a certain extent, have had influence abroad: the newspaper *El País*, whose first issue was published on May 4, 1976, and the radio network Cadena SER, created in 1924 and in which Prisa has had a majority stake since 1985. Meanwhile, the educational field is highlighted by the historical performance of the Santillana publishing group (1960) and its Fundación Santillana (1979), a company integrated in Prisa in the year 2000,[1] which currently brings together a group of publishers dedicated to the publication of textbooks and educational content with presence in Spain, Latin America, Portugal, the United Kingdom, and the United States.

Coinciding with the establishment of the democratic regime in Spain after the death of dictator Francisco Franco (1975), numerous analysts see in *El País* and Cadena SER a commitment to a democratic, modern, Europeanist Spain, one which recognizes the diversity within Spanish society.

El País

As explained in Chapter 2, a major political event that shocked Spanish society at the time gave *El País* the opportunity to position itself on the right side of history. We are referring to the Spanish coup d'état attempt on Monday, February 23, 1981 (known as 23-F or the Tejerazo), when Spain took its first steps toward democracy. Faced with an event of such magnitude, workers at the Prisa newspaper demonstrated their commitment to young democracy. *El País*, which at the time presented itself under the slogan *morning independent newspaper*, later published a 16-page special edition with a cover story titled "El País, con la Constitución". It was the way that the newspaper publicly condemned the coup d'état that hours later would reveal itself to be frustrated. In times of institutional turmoil, the editorial was forceful in stating that "the rebellion must be aborted; its accomplices and cover-ups, unmasked and put in safekeeping; and its authors, arrested, judged by courts that ensure a trial that is both impartial" (EL PAÍS, 1981).

From then on, Prisa's flagship publication would seek to be associated, and would indeed become associated, with contemporary democratic Spain. With the special edition of 23-F, Prisa set in motion a sort of sought-after specular game through which the header (*El País*) identified itself with Spain (the country) and vice versa. In other words, Spain would be reflected in the newspaper *El País*, while the newspaper *El País* would be the reflection of modern contemporary Spain.

Antonio Espantaleón Peralta, who in his work *El País y la transición política* (2002) analyzes the first years' performance of the newspaper, points out:

> If we classify the newspaper's editorials, from its beginnings to the first quarter of 1981 (Tejero's coup), and correlate them with the country's political dynamics, we can see a certain overlap between *El País* and the real country. A dynamic relationship that mutually reinforced each other.
>
> (Espantaleón Peralta, 2002: 20)

Years later, towards the end of 2017, Grupo Prisa took advantage of the end of the first four decades of democracy in Spain – coinciding with the 40th anniversary of *El País* – to launch, through its headline, the *España 40-40* cycle, explaining to its readers that

> *El País* has witnessed and participated in this transformation and wants to commemorate this anniversary by promoting a conversation, not only to reflect on these 40 years of democracy, but also to consider what the challenges are in the next four decades. To this end, it will count on the participation of opinion leaders from the social, cultural, economic and political spheres, who will analyse the dimension and role of Spain in Europe and in the world through different formats.
>
> (EL PAÍS, 2017c)

On the occasion of the 35th anniversary of the attempted coup d'état, Prisa Video produced a documentary, with script and direction by Daniel Cebrián (son of Juan Luis Cebrián, executive president of Grupo Prisa during 2008–2018), which bears the same title as the editorial of that historic and celebrated special issue of *El País*: *El País con la Constitución* (2016). Throughout its 75 minutes, the documentary recreates the hours of anxiety of that day inside the publishing house, emphasizing the decision of the then director, Juan Luis Cebrián, to make a special edition of El País, while the Chamber of Deputies was taken by military commanders. It also shows the voluntary participation of the company's workers and the national and international impact that the newspaper's extraordinary edition had. In the course of the documentary, Soledad Álvarez-Coto, then head of the national section, declares something that forms part of the journalistic editor's DNA: "In my opinion, 23-F is the most important moment in *El País* in all its years of history".

74 Cultural Profile

Ten years after publishing its first issue, the *El País* phenomenon gained an exhaustive analysis through the work coordinated by Gérard Imbert and José Vidal Beneyto: *El País o la referencia dominante* (1986). In that book, Prisa's daily newspaper is categorized as a "dominant reference newspaper", along with titles such as *La Repubblica* (Italy), *The Guardian* (UK), *O Estadão* (Brazil), and *The New York Times* (US). In this respect Imbert (in Imbert and Vidal Beneyto, 1986: 25) points out:

> Ten years after its creation, *El País* is already history. It has established itself as the dominant, unavoidable, obligatory reference for any political or cultural approach to the analysis of the Spanish reality of post-Francoism. It has a history, to have imposed itself as the first newspaper both nationally and internationally; a history of its own (with its internal struggles, its stages). Its revolution, its editorial twists, its critical-supports, positive criticisms, sermons and verdicts are intimately linked to the political evolution of the country and score the different governments of UCD [Union of Democratic Centre] and the three years of permanence in power of the socialists. *El País* has become a kind of formal representative of a public opinion that, on the other hand, it has contributed to form; it has become, in some critical moments, the almost exclusive guardian of the democratic spirit and, informally, it has sometimes assumed the role of alter ego of power, of mentor of the new political class. . . . *El País* has created and imposed a voice, often identified, in its editorial discourse, with the collective voice. How can an information apparatus, apart from its intrinsic quality and the undeniable professionalism of its members, in such a short time, and almost since its appearance, become a factory of references, cultural guidelines, a centre for the production of models, and occupy a privileged position in the production of sources of knowledge and opinion?

In general terms, it could be said that through the first years of action of the newspaper *El País*, to which Cadena SER would be added, Grupo Prisa was identified by its ideological orientation of centre-left, close at many junctures to the positions defended by the Spanish Socialist Workers' Party (PSOE). As we have seen in Chapter 1, the successive governments of the socialist Felipe González (1982–1996) and later the governments of José Luis Rodríguez Zapatero (2004–2011) would enable Prisa to successfully pursue its aggressive media diversification strategy.

Although for some information professionals *El País* continues to be a bastion of Spanish-language journalism and a key figure in contemporary Spain, it is no longer what it used to be. The four years in which *El País* was under the direction of Antonio Caño (2014–2018), who was close to

Juan Luis Cebrián, gave Prisa's newspaper a profile resembling that of the ideological right. The then correspondent of the newspaper in Washington arrived in Madrid with the idea that the newspaper "should open up to new majorities". This proclaimed opening was concretized, for example, in positions related to the government of Mariano Rajoy and, at the time, to the Ciudadanos political party: an informative treatment favourable to the Spanish Royal House when the institution had its worst moments, editorials against the new left wing political formation Podemos, and increasingly hostile coverage of the Catalan independence movement.

The ideological shift to the right of the traditional social democratic newspaper caused concern and rejection from much of the newsroom and its readers. It should be noted that with Caño's arrival, both the second editor (and current deputy editor of the newspaper) Joaquín Estefanía and one of the founding journalists (and current editor) Soledad Gallego-Díaz left the editorial board of *El País*. Both of these professionals were seen in the company as "the last presence of the values that were turning the newspaper into the reference that it became" (Gálvez, 2014). Caño's term at the head of the newspaper was peppered with clashes between the editorial board and the management due to "complaints from journalists about manipulation of their information and the general disengagement between the editorial staff and the editorial line of the newspaper" (Gálvez, 2014).

Towards the end of 2015, the veteran journalist Miguel Ángel Aguilar, who had an opinion column in the newspaper since 1994, was fired on the spot after his criticisms of the situation in the main Spanish newspapers, including *El País*, which appeared in an article published by *The New York Times*. In addition to pointing out that "[t]he newspapers are in the hands of creditors, and also in those of a government that has helped convince the creditors that the papers should be kept alive rather than just asphyxiated because of their debts", Aguilar asserted that: "Working at *El País* used to be the dream of any Spanish journalist. But now there are people so exasperated that they're leaving, sometimes even with the feeling that the situation has reached levels of censorship" (Minder, 2015).

In this article, signed by Raphael Minder (2015), it was reported that:

> The newspaper's editor, Antonio Caño, recently quashed an attempt by members of its newsroom committee to organize a vote of confidence over his leadership.
>
> In recent months, the newsroom committee raised concerns over articles that were altered or removed from the *El País* website after their publication, including two articles relating to Qatar, according to the minutes of the committee's internal meetings, which were seen by *The New York Times*.

Prisa, the parent company of *El País*, has been negotiating an investment from a Qatari company.

Another two articles concerned Telefónica, a company that is a shareholder of Prisa and that bought its television assets last year, helping Prisa cut its debt to 1.9 billion euros, or about $2.1 billion.

Last week, Mr. Caño, *El País*'s editor, said during a presentation that Prisa's debt "in no way" affected his paper's editorial content. Juan Luis Cebrián, the executive chairman of Prisa and co-founder of *El País*, also stressed newsroom independence. "What gets published is what the editor of El País wants to publish", he said.

Aside from the cessation of Aguilar's collaborations, the Asociación de Editores de Diarios Españoles (AEDE), which represents the publishers of 80 national and local newspapers and then presided over by Prisa CEO José Luis Sainz, accused *The New York Times* report of being "a caricature of Spanish news reality" (EL PAÍS, 2015). For its part, *El País* published the article "Los problemas económicos limitan la expansión de *The New York Times*" ("Economic problems limit the expansion of *The New York Times*"), in which it was reported that this newspaper had fired more than 300 journalists since 2008 and had a debt of 430 million dollars, calling into question its capacity to "maintain its independent editorial line" (Mars and Martínez Ahrens, 2015). Likewise, *El País* decided to stop offering the supplement of the American daily newspaper that it had been distributing weekly since 2004 – every Thursday a booklet was included with a selection of topics from *The New York Times* in Spanish (Soteras, 2015). In response, *The New York Times* spokeswoman, Eileen Murphy, lamented that *El País* used its pages "to carry out a kind of corporate vendetta" (C.L.B., 2015).

Some months after the clash with *The New York Times*, the outbreak of the Panama Papers scandal – which gave rise to several reports linking Juan Luis Cebrián to the oil company Star Petroleum of Iranian businessman Massoud Zandi (see later the suspension of the collaborations of journalist Ignacio Escolar in Cadena SER) – caused discomfort among several professionals from *El País* and Cadena SER. "Cebrián is a tyrant like Calígula" was the hidden message that could be read in the opinion note of the *El País*'s supplement Tentaciones, signed by Juan Soto Ivars. The young writer and journalist publicly justified why he decided to "tell Cebrián what I think of him in his own home" (Soto Ivars, 2016):

> Because I grew up reading *El País*, I was educated reading *El País* and I got to know Spain reading *El País*; because I have been watching for years how they turn a newspaper full of excellent professionals into a farmhouse at the service of their creditor. I don't want what I've done

to be understood as an attack on the newspaper, because it's a defence. I really want *El País* to go back to what it was.

The dynamics of Spanish politics and the changes in Grupo Prisa and its media go hand in hand. And the era of Cebrián-Caño seemed to be over at the end of 2018. The motion of censure that in 2018 removed Rajoy from the government and catapulted the socialist Pedro Sánchez would have its correlate in the direction of *El País*: Soledad Gallego-Díaz replaced Caño.

Two months before the changeover, the journalist Fernando Cano (2018) anticipated the play in the pages of *El Español*:

> Prisa's majority shareholders are convinced that *El País* . . . must make a left turn and recover its historical roots. A strategy that necessarily involves replacing Antonio Caño. . . . It is not a question of returning to Felipe González's old PSOE, nor of throwing oneself into the arms of the new left represented by Podemos, but of turning the wheel and moving away from the profile close to the ideological right that has been printed on the head of Caño. . . . The objective is for *El País* to cease being subject to political and business powers and to remove the "institutional" poster that it has been cultivating for years, replacing it with a more independent profile.
>
> We are talking about an ideological turn for commercial reasons, as it is a matter of satisfying historical readers again, but also the new generations who see *El País* as a bourgeois capital and close to power, quite the opposite of the values he cultivated forty years ago with his birth. It is a question of gaining more readers, and therefore of increasing incomes.

Indeed, the changes in the top management of Grupo Prisa and the departure of Cebrián as president of the company precipitated the move away from Caño. With the appointment of Soledad Gallego-Díaz, the first woman at the head of *El País* in its four decades of history,[2] some considered Prisa's management to somehow seek to return to the essence of the newspaper, recovering the former ideological profile – a centre-left editorial line – and offer content more in line with the interests of *El País*'s readers. The appointment of Gallego-Díaz, backed by 97.2 per cent of the votes of the newspaper's workforce, supports this idea of a bid to return to the historic social democratic line from the hand of a professional of the old guard (PÚBLICO/AGENCIAS, 2018).

Indeed, under the direction of the new female director, *El País* launched the "¿Y tu qué piensas?" (And what do you think?) campaign at the beginning of 2019, developed by the brand department of Prisa Noticias and the advertising agency Shackleton. The campaign directly appealed to its readers and proclaims *El País* as "A space to understand. Also, to think", highlighting "the values that have accompanied the newspaper since its foundation", focusing on five major themes: immigration, feminism, education, ecology, and dialogue (EL PAÍS, 2017a).

However, and in spite of the major themes proclaimed, the editorial line of the newspaper after Gallego-Díaz's appointment barely underwent any change in terms of major political issues like the coverage of the Podemos political party or support for the Crown and the 1978 Constitution.

Finally, there are two issues that in recent years have shaken (and still shake) the life of *El País*: on the one hand, the removal of advertisements in the pages of the newspaper that encourage prostitution and, on the other, the journalistic coverage of the bullfights that take place in the main venues of the country.

Regarding the first of these questions, on July 15, 2017, *El País* stopped publishing the so-called contact advertisements, advertisements that encouraged sexual exploitation mainly of women. This historic step was taken in order to ensure the editorial coherence of this Prisa outlet. Evidently, it could not be understood that the profuse coverage by *El País* about male violence and its most serious consequence (i.e., gender violence) shared space with this type of advertisement. The decision was made after numerous complaints accumulated by the *defensor del lector* of *El País* (many readers did not understand how a socially progressive newspaper and defender of human values promoted prostitution) and a decade after various Spanish media (such as *Público, La Gaceta, 20 Minutos*, or *La Razón*) had suppressed this type of advertising. It was estimated that the decision to give up a secure and substantial source of income meant that the publisher of *El País* stopped earning between 12,000 and 14,000 euros per day (DIRCONFIDENCIAL, 2017).

Complementing this action, it should be noted that in May 2018, *El País* announced the creation of a gender correspondent, with the objective of "planning and improving current coverage on issues related to equality and women" (El PAÍS, 2018a). Subsequently, in June 2018, the first female correspondent to tackle this assignment arrived at the paper.

In relation to the journalistic coverage of bullfighting events by *El País* (and the radio network Cadena SER of Grupo Prisa), it should be noted that Spain is the country par excellence of bullfighting. Bullfights, held in this country since the twelfth century, have been considered not only a commercial and leisure activity, but also a political event (Schubert, 2002). Despite this historical tradition, in recent years there has been a growing rejection in various sectors of Spanish society towards the celebration of popular festivities in which bulls are used (*encierros, bous, suelta de reses*, etc.) as well as festivities of bullfights (bullfights, *rejones, recortes* contests, etc.). The anti-bullfighters claim that bullfights are cruel and wild events that offend sensitivity and civic sense. For their part, lovers of bullfights recognize in these an ancestral spectacle part of Spain's cultural heritage. In this sense, the Spanish philosopher Fernando Savater, linked to *El País* since the beginning of the newspaper, points out that bullfights are "a game of undoubted literary and artistic roots, codified and stylized rigorously over the centuries, enjoyed by many people and guarantees a way of life and a type of economic development, linked to the landscape and livestock" (Savater, 2011).

In this context, for decades there has been a debate led by some of the readers of *El País* who believe that this journalistic medium should stop covering bullfighting. *El País*, which has columnists for and against bullfights, has not shied away from the debate. When in the summer of 2010 the Catalan Parliament approved the ban on bullfighting in Catalonia starting in 2012, *El País* was one of a group of generalist newspapers – along with *La Vanguardia*, *El Periódico de Catalunya*, and *Avui* (all published in Catalonia) – that included journalistic coverage in favour of the ban (Urchaga Litago *et al.*, 2017). And in September 2017, it set up an online, non-scientific survey to obtain the opinion of its readers, which received 37,486 responses. On this occasion 60.6 per cent of the participants expressed their belief that bullfighting festivities would disappear and 58.66 per cent were in favour of banning them (EL PAÍS, 2017d).

In mid-2019 the current *defensor del lector*, Carlos Yárnoz, left a record of *El País*'s position. In his Sunday column he denied that the time had come to stop publishing bullfighting chronicles, supporting this refusal by appealing to the arguments put forward by its editor in chief of the culture section: "Since its foundation, the newspaper has bet on considering bullfighting as a cultural spectacle". He also made it clear that "only critiques of large fairs are published 'because of their social repercussions' and that this 'cultural dimension' is reflected in chronicles with 'literary overtones'" (Yárnoz, 2019).

Cadena SER: The Voice of Prisa

Parallel to the failed attempt to consolidate its own radio offer through Radio El País (1983–1987), in 1983 Grupo Prisa became a shareholder of Spain's oldest private radio network: Cadena SER. Cadena SER's programs – which encompass news, sports, talk, entertainment, and culture – can be accessed throughout Spain. The network's main studios are located on the Gran Vía street in central Madrid. In addition, studios across the country contribute local and regional news and information, with local programming in each location amounting to between 2 and 3.5 hours daily.

Throughout its decades of operation, Cadena SER has had the capacity to create emblematic radio programs that have achieved relevance and sustained

80   Cultural Profile

continued presence. Such are the cases of the great news programs that today form the backbone of the editorial and informative line of this channel: *Hoy por hoy* and *Hora 25*. The first of these is a news and current affairs morning program, which began broadcasting on September 22, 1986, and was directed and presented by the renowned journalist and political analyst Iñaki Gabilondo for nearly two decades (1986–2005). It should be noted that *Hoy por hoy* has several minutes of local programming broadcasted by Cadena SER owned and operated and affiliated stations in Spain (from 12:20 pm to 2 pm) and that the format was exported to Radio Caracol (Colombia), for example.

For its part, *Hora 25* is the program that since 1972 occupies the night hours of Cadena SER (Monday to Friday, from 8 pm to 11:30 pm) and is dedicated to the informative analysis of the events that took place during the day.[3] Late journalist Carlos Llamas was the director-presenter of this program for 15 years, between 1992 and 2006, and led the program to leadership in its time slot. There is a shorter edition called *Hora 25-Fin de semana* that is broadcast on Sundays (from 11 pm to 11:30 pm).

Other current emblematic programs of Cadena SER are *La ventana* and *A vivir que son dos días*. The first of these, created in 1993 and broadcast in the afternoons (from 4 pm to 8 pm), is a program of current affairs, interviews, and humour. It was directed and presented by journalist Gemma Nierga for 15 years (1997–2012). The program has some minutes of local programming broadcasted by Cadena SER owned and operated and affiliated stations from Monday to Friday (from 7:20 pm to 7:40 pm). Prisa Radio has exported *La ventana* to other radio stations in the group, such as Radio Panamá (Panama) and Radio Caracol (Colombia). On the other hand, *A vivir que son dos días* was premiered in Spain on March 12, 1988, with an interview with then vice-president of the government Alfonso Guerra (PSOE). Currently, this variety and entertainment program is broadcast in Spain on weekends (Saturdays and Sundays from 8 am to 12 pm). The program/format was exported to Colombia and Argentina through Prisa Radio Caracol and Radio Continental.

In the field of sports programming, there is *Carrousell deportivo*, Spain's oldest radio program dating to 1952, and *El larguero*, on air since 1989. These are two programs that connect with one of the most widespread passions among Spaniards, namely, football, a sport introduced by English labourers who worked for the Rio Tinto mining company in Huelva at the end of the nineteenth century. It should be noted that Spain has one of the most competitive professional leagues in the world (officially the National First Division League Championship) involving internationally renowned teams (Barcelona FC and Real Madrid CF) and that the Spanish men's team won the 2010 World Cup in South Africa. *Carrousell deportivo*, a program that is usually compared to *5 live Sport* (the flagship banner of live rolling sports block on BBC Radio 5 Live), is transmitted on weekends (from 3 pm to 1:30 am)

Cultural Profile 81

and on Sundays (from 12 pm to 2:30 pm), covering football games of the Spanish La Liga premier division and analyzing the day's sports news. This program also covers UEFA Champions League games, the UEFA Cup, and Spanish national football team matches. For its part, *El larguero*, broadcast daily (from 11:30 pm to 1:30 am), is concentrated mostly on football discussion sports results, interviews, and sports analysis.

In addition to the always remembered role played by Cadena SER during the failed coup attempt of 23-F in 1981, when it had not yet been acquired by Grupo Prisa, the radio network had the opportunity to validate its commitment to truthful information and its audience on the occasion of the attacks perpetrated on 11-M of 2004 in the capital of Spain. The attacks on four trains of the Madrid suburban network carried out by a Al Qaeda type terrorist cell, which left 191 people dead and around 1,800 wounded, occurred 72 hours after the opening of the ballot boxes to hold general elections.

Cadena SER played a leading role during the days following the most serious terrorist attacks in the history of Spain by dismantling the information strategy of the government of José María Aznar (PP), who attributed the attack to the Basque terrorist group ETA (an acronym for Euskadi Ta Askatasuna, which can be translated as Basque Homeland and Liberty, or Basque Country and Freedom). Unlike the public media – such as the news agency Efe and the television stations TVE (national) and Telemadrid (regional) – the information from Cadena SER was key to questioning the allegations of the Aznar administration, which had added Spain to the international coalition that occupied Iraq (2003–2011) and overthrew Saddam Hussein. As with *El País*, Cadena SER is identified by its proximity to the PSOE's interests, although it is true that during the government of the socialist Rodríguez Zapatero (2004–2011) there has been a certain divergence between the actions of this administration and the editorial line of the radio station.

Alejandro Nieto, radio producer for Grupo Caracol Radio (Colombia), was the person designated by Prisa to carry out the most important personnel restructuring in a radio group in Spain in recent years. Accompanying Nieto in his position as general director of Cadena SER (2010–2015) was journalist Antonio Hernández-Rodicio as director of Informative Services (2011–2013) and director of Cadena SER (2013–2018). Indeed, Hernández-Rodicio was responsible for initiating the most important editorial change experienced by Grupo Prisa's radio network in recent decades: the alignment with the editorial lines marked by José Luis Cebrián, Antonio Caño, and David Alandete (former deputy director of *El País*, 2014–2018), among others.[4]

In April 2016, one of the most controversial episodes in recent years took place that undermined the credibility and prestige of Grupo Prisa's main radio network: the expulsion from Cadena SER of Ignacio Escolar, the director of the digital newspaper *eldiario.es* who had been working as a political analyst on the program *Hoy por hoy*. The expulsion of Escolar, decided by then Prisa's CEO Juan Luis Cebrián, was motivated by the fact that *eldiario.es* and other media – *ElConfidencial.com* and the television station La Sexta – published information that linked Cebrián to the Panama Papers. The Papers contained evidence that Cebrián's wife at the time, Teresa Aranda, appeared as a proxy for Granite Corporation, a company with front men from the Seychelles-based firm Mossack Fonseca, and that Cebrián owned 2 per cent of the Luxembourg oil company Star Petroleum, which he would have obtained by a donation made through an offshore company from Iranian-born businessman Massoud Farshad Zandi.

Before his dismissal from *Hoy por hoy*,[5] Escolar reflected:

> With my case, we have seen what freedom of expression means to those who have been one of the best journalists in the history of Spain, Juan Luis Cebrián, the founder of *El País* . . . [a person] who doesn't recognize himself with the newspaper he founded or with the journalist he was.[6]

For its part, the Madrid Press Association (APM, 2016) issued a statement on the occasion of World Press Freedom Day in which it said that:

> The freedom of the press is attacked and resented when any power, whatever it may be, tries to intimidate information professionals so that their chronicles acquire a bias more convenient to their interests, regardless of whether that bias responds or not to the truth of the facts or the professional judgement of the journalist.
>
> It resents and is attacked when retaliation is exercised against journalists who publish information that bothers or denounces those who have the capacity and power to retaliate against them, even if that information is truthful and duly accredited.

Accompanying the expulsion of Escolar were the legal actions taken by Cebrián in his name and in Prisa's name against *eldiario.es*, *ElConfidencial.com*, and La Sexta television channel, the prohibition on journalists from the group collaborating with these media, and the order that Prisa's media truncate in their news any link between Cebrián and the Panama Papers.

While Cadena SER's shift to the right was not as abrupt as that of *El País*, today Cadena SER is seeking to relocate to the ideological bias. Thus, at the beginning of 2018 there were important changes in Cadena SER's organization, forming "a truffled organigram of well-known names in the house with which the new Prisa intends to return to its origins after some complicated years that many want to leave behind" (Zarzalejos, 2018).

Apart from the protagonism of the talk radio of Prisa, which was always in the media-political epicentre, it exhibits a very active front in the field of musical radio with several networks dedicated to different styles. These include Los 40 (formerly Los 40 Principales) and Cadena Dial. The first of these is a Top 40 musical radio network and radio station brand in many Spanish-speaking countries from Prisa Radio. The station has its origins in a music show at Radio Madrid, today Cadena SER, in 1966, where the 40 Principales chart was born, then evolved into a standalone radio station in 1979. This radio format was exported to Latin American countries, and today Los 40 stations broadcast in Argentina, Chile, Colombia, Costa Rica, the Dominican Republic, Ecuador, Mexico (franchised to Televisa Radio and aired by many Radiorama stations), Paraguay, and Panama. For its part, Cadena Dial, whose central studios are located in Madrid, although it has frequencies distributed throughout the Spanish territory, has broadcast pop music in Spanish exclusively since September 1990.

By the end of 2019, Prisa had four state-wide music networks in Spain: Los 40 and its two little sisters, Los 40 Classic (formerly M80, 1993–2018) and Los 40 Dance (formerly Máxima FM, 2002–2019), plus the successful Cadena Dial, which enjoys an outstanding commercial target among middle-aged audiences. In addition to these music radio networks, there are three other small, low-cost music networks: Radiolé, dedicated to *cañí* folklore (*copla, rumba, flamenco,* and *sevillanas*) and based mainly in the south of the country; Kebuena, a thematic radio station that relies on reggaeton (also found in Mexico); and Clásica FM, the successor to Sinfo Radio, which survives on the Internet.

At present, the programs of Cadena SER as well as those of Los 40 and Cadena Dial can be listened to through FM radio, Spanish digital terrestrial television (DTT), the Internet, and apps for mobile devices. Aware of the changes that give prominence to the interaction between people and technological devices through voice (for example, intelligent loudspeakers), the present strategy of Grupo Prisa in relation to its offerings in audio content is not anchored in the traditional "making radio", but in "producing the best audio content . . . taking advantage of the power of brands such as [Cadena] SER, Caracol, or Los 40" (Jiménez and Delgado, 2019a).

Finally, in mid-2016 in Madrid, Prisa launched Prisa Radio's global Spanish podcast network: Podium Podcast. The four pillars of Podium's catalogue are fiction, journalism, entertainment, and the so-called essentials, based on the recovery of the best of Prisa Radio's archive. Podium premiered with some 20 programs with exclusive and free content. Prisa stations in Colombia, Chile, Argentina, and Mexico have a prominent place in the project, both in terms of broadcasting and content creation.

"Sonajero" by Fisher-Price (manufacturer of toys for preschool children), "Pienso, luego actúo" by Yoigo (mobile phones), "Aerolínea Momentos" by Iberia (Spanish airline), "Ruido blanco" by Greenpeace, "100 años en

84 *Cultural Profile*

Metro" by Metro de Madrid, "En la cabeza de Carlos Soria" by Correos (Spanish postal service operator), and "Abrimos la ópera" by Endesa (electricity company) are just some of the branded podcast projects, among more than a dozen, that have been created so far by Podium Podcast.

After its first three years of operation and in a context marked by the growth in audio consumption, Grupo Prisa is striving to make Podium Podcast profitable. In June 2019 the Podium Studios of Prisa Radio debuted. It is an audio production company that offers the group's brands a range of possibilities within the universe of digital audio. Podium Studios offers branded podcasts, smart speaker applications, audio marketing (audiologists, audio-branding, and sound identities), corporate podcasts, and support in the distribution and promotion of podcasts.

Editorial Santillana

It is often pointed out that Santillana is the jewel in Prisa's crown, as this publishing company dedicated to *creating value in education* – such is its current motto – contributed in 2018 almost 50 per cent of the company's income and has a presence in virtually every country in Latin America. Santillana is a company that expects to achieve "organic growth of over 10 per cent [in 2019], with remarkable results in countries . . . such as Brazil, Spain, Mexico, and Colombia", according to statements made by CEO Miguel Ángel Cayuela to *El País* (Jiménez and Delgado, 2019b).

As stated in Chapter 3, devoted to the economic analysis of Grupo Prisa, Santillana's corporate report for 2019 highlights the international presence of this company, which has a team of 3,989 employees who provide educational services and solutions in 21 countries. Likewise, the report shows the current far-reaching scope of the company: in 2018, 32 million students used Santillana's educational resources and services; 93.7 million textbooks were sold; 25,000 classrooms were computerized; and Santillana's brands had almost three million followers on social networks.

Founded in 1960 by Jesús Polanco, Francisco Pérez González, and Juan A. Cortés, Santillana joined Grupo Prisa in 2000. The fact that it holds the title of crown jewel is related to the particular functioning of the non-university textbook sector for formal education in several of the countries where Santillana operates. In Spain, for example, the marketing of textbooks has peculiar characteristics. The families of the students are able to select books according to their sale prices, since they are obliged to acquire those books prescribed by the educational centre their children attend. On the other hand, it should be pointed out that there are fixed-price educational stages (infant education, high school, and vocational training) and others that are free (primary education and compulsory secondary education). To this must be added a very clear and determinant regulation on the contents of these books and schools have a legal obligation to maintain the same books for periods of at least four years.

This is a relatively stable business where it is key to have established relations with the public administrations of each country as well as to "know well the local markets and adapt the pedagogical contents and services to the curricular needs and idiosyncrasies of each country", according to statements by Francisco Cuadrado, former Global Director of Education of Santillana (Manrique Sagobal, 2016). The weight of exports is not significant since the idea is to print and sell books whose contents are adapted to the curricular needs of each country. In Latin American markets, which together accounted for more than 82 per cent of Santillana's revenue in 2014 (Manrique Sabogal, 2016), the company has been competing with other large publishing houses with numerous subsidiaries such as Grupo Océano, Grupo Editorial Norma (as noted, acquired by Santillana in 2016), Grupo Planeta, McGraw-Hill, and Pearson Education (Enríquez Fuentes, 2008: 9).

For example, a report by the Observatory of Cultural Policies (OCP) of Chile's National Council for Culture and the Arts (August 2012) notes that according to data from Chile's Ministry of Education – the state's main purchaser of books – both investment in school textbooks and the number of textbooks purchased increased over the years. Regarding market share in the Ministry of Education's textbook award, the report notes that Santillana had a significant share in the 2007–2010 period (around 20 per cent of the total). In 2010, Santillana accounted for 43 per cent of the total market, followed by Colombia's Norma (14 per cent) and Chile's Cal y Canto (14 per cent) and MN (12 per cent) (OCP, 2012: 25).

In Mexico, the country with the highest number of Spanish speakers (at the beginning of the century it already had more than 100 million inhabitants), the National Commission for Free Textbooks (Conaliteg is the abbreviation in Spanish) was founded in 1959 as part of the national mandate to provide Mexicans with free and compulsory education. Sixty years later, this decentralized public agency produces and distributes, for each school year and free of charge, textbooks and materials determined by the Secretary of Public Education (SEP), which are required for students enrolled in the national education system. Five of the ten main companies contracted by Conaliteg during the term of President Enrique Peña Nieto (2012–2018) were foreign: Editorial Santillana, Richmond Publishing (belonging to Santillana and specializing in publishing books and materials that facilitate the process of learning the English language), SM de Ediciones (founded in 1938 in Spain by the Marianist family, a missionary group of María that owns SM companies, with presence in several Latin American countries), Macmillan Publishers (German publishing group Georg von Holtzbrinck Gmbh), and

Ediciones Castillo (belonging to MacMillan Education Company). The largest book purchase contract of Peña Nieto's government was a direct award to Editorial Santillana for more than 6.5 million dollars, for the acquisition of 466 titles for the 2018–2019 secondary program of free textbooks. For its part, Richmond Publishing received 71 awards with Conaliteg in the six years of Peña Nieto for a value of 1.26 million dollars. This is how a Spanish group, through Mexican subsidiaries, obtained just over 52.6 million dollars in six years for contracts with Conaliteg (Granados Arocha/PODER, 2019).

Apart from its performance in the educational sector, Santillana's activity in the years when the company entered the field of fiction and literature was underpinned by Babelia, the weekly supplement of *El País* dedicated to the evolution of the different cultural disciplines, which has been in print since 1991 and in which Latin American literature and newly published works have a prominent place. In literary circles, one still recalls the controversy derived from a very negative 2004 review of a novel edited by Alfaguara (*El hijo del acordeonista*, by Bernardo Atxaga) by the literary critic Ignacio Echevarría in the pages of Babelia. The Echevarría-Babelia case called into question the credibility of *El País* when the interests of the business group collided with an independent critic, which aroused the concern of numerous collaborators of *El País*.[7]

It should be noted that in its years of strong expansion and diversification of activities, and directly linked to editorial production, Prisa established its own chain of bookstores called Crisol. In addition to the sale of books, music, and films, many of Crisol's branches were multicultural spaces that served as a platform for the presentation and promotion of writers, through the signing of books, gatherings, and conferences. Its heyday came in the mid-1990s, when 17 stores were opened: 14 in Spain, in the cities of Barcelona, Seville, Valencia, and Madrid; two in the city of Buenos Aires, Argentina; and one in Lima, Peru. However, at the end of the first decade of the twenty-first century, the last three stores of the Crisol chain closed due to "the current economic slowdown, the reorientation, or almost disappearance, of the music and video businesses" and the "major changes in the sector, such as greater sales in large stores or the expansion of other spaces such as the [network of bookstores] Casa del Libro, or the establishment in Spain of Fnac [a large French retail chain selling cultural and electronic products]" (Gaviña, 2009).

Santillana's adventure in the field of fiction and literature publishing culminated in mid-2014, when Grupo Prisa, under the weight of pressing debt, closed the sale of all the shares of its subsidiary Santillana Ediciones Generales, which included publishing houses in Spain and Portugal/Brazil, to Penguin Random House, the global trade book publisher owned 75 per cent by Bertelsmann (Germany) and 25 per cent by Pearson (UK). This sale meant that Santillana got rid of imprints such as Alfaguara, Taurus, Aguilar,

Suma de Letras, Punto de Lectura, Altea, Fontanar, Objetiva, and Foglio (the latter three in Brazil) that include in their catalogues authors such as José Saramago (Nobel Prize for Literature 1998), Günter Grass (Nobel Prize for Literature 1999), Mario Vargas Llosa (Nobel Prize for Literature 2000), Jorge Luis Borges, Guillermo Cabrera Infante, Isabel Allende, and Arturo Pérez-Reverte.

Santillana justified the loss of this prestigious symbolic (and economic) capital with the following statement:

> With this operation, Santillana will fully focus its activity in the area of education, immersed in a digital and pedagogical transformation that responds to the different educational realities of the countries where the company operates. In 2013, education contributed 87 per cent of the company's income.
>
> (PRISA, 2014)

Grupo Prisa's abandonment of the field of fiction and literature publishing has left the Spanish conglomerate Grupo Planeta – acting in different business areas (through the company Planeta DeAgostini is a reference shareholder of Atresmedia, a Spanish communications group with television and radio stations) apart from the publishing sector, where it owns the publishing houses Planeta, Espasa, Seix-Barral, Austral, Paidós, Ariel, Crítica, Minotauro, etc. – as the main competitor of Penguin Random House in the Spanish language market.

Having abandoned the field of literary publishing, Santillana, which during 2010–2019 was 25 per cent owned by the venture capital fund DLJ South American Partners, was at the end of this period focusing on textbook publishing and educational content once again. In Spain, for example, the replacement of textbooks in primary education (EP) and compulsory secondary education (ESO) by the controversial Organic Law for the Improvement of Educational Quality (LOMCE) enacted in 2013 under the mandate of Mariano Rajoy (2011–2018) boosted the publisher's revenues at a time of economic crisis in Prisa.

In the middle of this decade, in Spain, Santillana led the education segment with a market share of 19.3 per cent. It also held first place in the markets of Brazil (19.9 per cent), Mexico (17.4 per cent), Argentina (27.6 per cent), Chile (38.8 per cent), and Colombia (17.2 per cent). And in Portugal it was ranked the third leading company (7.1 per cent) in the education business (Ugalde, 2016).

The strong presence of Santillana and Prisa in the formation of the younger generations and in the construction of the contemporary historical account of Spain is evident, for example, in acts such as the one that took place at the end of 2018 in the Congress of Deputies on the occasion of the presentation of *La fabulosa historia de nuestra democracia* (*The Fabulous History of our Democracy*) (Grassa Toro, 2018), "a book with the objective of narrating to the younger generation how the Magna Carta arose and how Spain has changed in these 40 years" (Casqueiro, 2018).

Santillana's reputation, and that of the rest of Spain's leading non-university textbook publishers, was damaged in 2019 when the National Commission on Markets and Competition (CNMC in Spanish) sanctioned 34 textbook publishers and the Asociación Nacional de Editores de Libros y material de Enseñanza (ANELE) for engaging in two illicit behaviours (CNMC, 2019). First, through a code of conduct launched in 2012, publishers and ANELE homogenized their policies and commercial conditions in the sector in order to reduce and eliminate those elements that introduced competition in textbook prescribing. In this infringement, the CNMC alleged the involvement of a total of 33 companies, of which seven companies belonged to Santillana (Ediciones Grazalema, Edicions Obradoiro, Edicions Voramar, Grup Promotor D'Ensenyament, Grupo Santillana Educación Global, Santillana Educación S.L., and Zubia Editoriala). Second, the CNMC alleged that the marketers of the Santillana, SM, and Anaya publishing groups, together with Edebé, MacMillan, McGraw Hill, Oxford University Press, Pearson Education, the publishing house Teide, and Edición del Serbal, reached agreements and coordinated practices for the fixing of prices and other commercial conditions in relation to textbooks in digital format in Spain between 2014 and 2017. In this way, competition was restricted in relation to the marketing of a novel and expanding a product.

Finally, it should be noted that the development of comprehensive learning systems, with subscription models – such as Compartir, UNOi, and Educa – was in 2019 one of the company's main bets to ensure its growth. As Prisa's CEO, Manuel Mirat, points out, "this is not about selling textbooks to parents, but about a complete relationship with schools, through platforms and with three- or four-year contracts, which include a strong digital component, materials, advice" (Jiménez and Delgado, 2019a). Santillana has already implemented these systems and was developing them in more than 3,000 schools in 15 Latin American countries, and has approximately 1.4 million students on its platforms. As Miguel Ángel Cayuela (in Jiménez and Delgado, 2019b) points out,

> the ARPU [Average Revenue Per User] that we obtain with these systems is clearly superior to the traditional business. It is not a question of selling e-books, printed books or other tools in a disaggregated manner, but of offering ecosystems that seek greater consistency in our pedagogical proposal and in how it is implemented in the centres: LMS [Learning Management Systems] platforms that include content, evaluation tools, advice and training for teachers, technology. . . . The school is the engine

of educational transformation, and we believe that this integral proposal directly influences the educational improvement of its students and, therefore, offers greater value to the school. . . . [Comprehensive learning systems] [i]mply a longer-term relationship with the school and its teachers, as three- or four-year contracts are signed for all subjects. This allows us to give them a more personalized and richer offer, and to establish bonds of trust and mutual commitment with the schools in learning progress. We become, in a way, school consultants designing with them plans for continuous improvement. Internally, for Santillana it has meant a radical change in the way we work and in the profiles we need.

As the market for comprehensive learning systems consolidates,[8] Santillana's model is expected to become the main booster of Prisa's income. It is a business group that at the end of the second decade of the twenty-first century admits to not historically having had "a good story about education and everything it implies for this group". It is, moreover, a group that today places its media and education companies on an equal footing by emphasizing Prisa's mission "to improve society with quality educational products and credible media" (Jimenéz and Delgado, 2019a).

Social Acceptance of Grupo Prisa's Main Media

Referring to the presence of the Grupo Prisa's most popular products and services, understood as those that are most accepted by the public, implies talking about consumption. And here we return to *El País* and Cadena SER as outstanding Prisa showcases.

El País

El País has been the main media asset of Grupo Prisa since its birth. In its more than four decades of existence, this newspaper has gone from becoming a benchmark for journalism written in Spanish to giving priority to its market role on an international scale. This transformation has been apparent in the very motto of the newspaper, which has gone from being an *independent morning newspaper* during 1976–2007, to the later *global newspaper*, passing through *the global newspaper in Spanish*, for some years in between.

In June 1981, only a few years after its launch, *El País* had already become the national daily newspaper with the highest sales in Spain, surpassing historic newspapers such as *La Vanguardia* (published in Barcelona since 1881, entitled *La Vanguardia Española* between 1939 and 1978), *ABC* (published in Madrid since 1903), *Ya* (edited in Madrid during 1935–1996, founded by Editorial Católica, one of the most popular and influential newspapers in Spain during Franco's regime), *El Periódico* (published since 1978 in Barcelona), *Diario 16* (published in Madrid during 1976–2001),[9] *El Correo* (published in Bilbao since 1938), and *El Alcázar* (published in Madrid during 1936–1987) (EL PAÍS, 1982).

As Antonio Espantaleón Peralta (2002: 27) points out: "*El País*, taking into account our [Spanish] low readership rates, was read a lot from the beginning and soon became the newspaper with the largest circulation. And its 'validity' was much greater than its 'reading'".

With its head office and central editorial office in Madrid, the editor of *El País* has maintained offices in the main cities of Spain (Barcelona, Valencia, Seville, Bilbao, Santiago de Compostela, Algeciras), enclaves where different territorial editions are published – though the size and resources of these regional newsrooms have diminished over time because of the financial problems of the group. At the end of the last century, however, *El País* had 11 editions printed on the presses located in seven Spanish cities: Madrid, Barcelona, Valencia, Seville, Lugo, Burgos, and Las Palmas. In addition, three other editions were printed: one in Frankfurt (Germany) and another in Heerlen (Holland) for Europe, and one in Mexico City for America (EL PAÍS, 1999).

In 1992, the newspaper sold more than 400,000 copies a day (sales at kiosks plus subscriptions) in a market that at that time had a total population of 39.2 million inhabitants. In other words, in little more than a decade, *El País* doubled its sales. The ascent continued and towards the end of the 1990s Prisa's newspaper, which has had an online version since 1996, sold more than 450,000 copies a day (see Figure 5.1).

It would be in the middle of the first decade of the twenty-first century, and in a context of growing Internet penetration, when *El País* reached its best sales year in its first 44 years of history: in 2004, in a territory populated by 43.2 million inhabitants, it reached a circulation of 469,183 copies per day. That year, *El País* surpassed the second Spanish newspaper in the sales ranking, *El Mundo*, by 160,954 copies, and *ABC*, which ranked third, by 192,268 copies.

Although a little more than three decades have passed since then, in 2020, these figures look very distant, since after 2004 the newspaper's sales collapsed. *El País* closed 2018 with a total circulation (the sum of kiosk sales, individual and collective subscriptions, free copies, and other special channels) of 137,552 copies: a remarkable 70.7 per cent drop from 14 years prior.

Several factors can be pointed out to explain this drastic drop in sales. On the one hand, there was an international context in which, in general terms, there is a decline in sales of newspapers printed on paper as opposed to the consumption of information through various digital channels. And, on the other hand, there were internal contextual factors, among which were a similar offering of informative content via the printed edition *El País*, paid for, and through the Internet, free of charge. There was also, of course, the economic crisis that broke out worldwide in 2008, but that particularly and severely affected

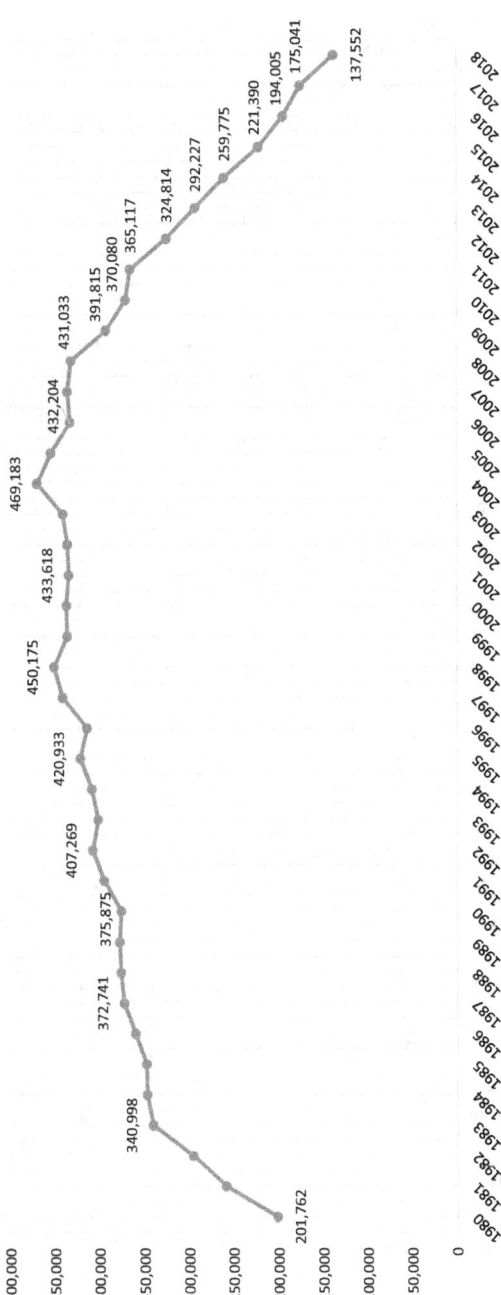

Figure 5.1 El País: Newspaper Sales Between 1980 and 2018

Source: OJD

Note: Spanish population reference: 1980: 37,493,072 inhabitants; 1986: 38,638,052; 1996: 39,971,329; 2006: 44,784,659; and 2016: 46,524,943 (source: INE)

consumption in Spain. Also, the ideological right turn exhibited by the daily may have taken a high toll in terms of readership, since pay readers of the printed versions usually had a higher level of commitment than online readers accessing the newspaper for free. However, or maybe because of it, the business model of the online version of *El País* has followed a rather turbulent path.

The acute crisis affecting Prisa's flagship publication led then director Antonio Caño (2014–2018) to send an open letter in March 2016 to the newspaper's editorial staff announcing the imminent transformation into an essentially digital newspaper. Although Caño assured that the newspaper would continue to be published on paper for as long as possible, his writing predicted the future disappearance of the printed edition because "the transfer of readers from paper to digital is constant" and because "the habit of buying the newspaper at the kiosk has been reduced to a minority" (Caño, 2016).

With the advent of the Internet, Prisa was one of the first publishers to launch a digital newspaper. On the 20th anniversary of the birth of *El País*, on May 4, 1996, *ElPaís.es* was launched, making *El País* online one of the founding digital newspapers of the Online Publishers Association-Europe, the European branch of the Association of Electronic Publishers. In a short time, the digital edition of *El País* was generating its own content, and despite a limited number of PCs in businesses and homes, gradually increasing its number of readers. In September 1999, *ElPaís.es* exhibited solid leadership, with 90,768 visits per day, well ahead of the second highest ranking site, *El Mundo*, with 46,836 visits (Seoane and Sueiro, 2004: 579).

Driven by this leadership and by the desire to turn the website into a new source of income, those responsible for the digital strategy of Prisa (Prisacom) decided, on November 18, 2002, to make the riskiest decision in the short life of *ElPaís.es*: to completely redesign it and turn it into a paid newspaper. Only a few areas of content (such as the front page and the editorials) and services continued to be freely accessible, setting up a kind of online shop window in search of customers. "The decision to opt for the subscription system to access the *ElPaís.es* website has not been easy, but we were obliged to look for a new source of income that would allow us to guarantee the evolution of the product with a view to the future", said then Prisacom Director of Content Mario Tascón (in Albornoz, 2007: 154).

The payment model didn't last long. In the middle of 2005, Prisa's directors were backing down and the digital edition of *El País* was once again free of charge (EL PAÍS, 2005). In a national and international context of digital press media written in Spanish with free access, the decision to set up a payment barrier did not have the expected effect. On the one hand, the economic expectations did not materialize (at the time of abandoning the payment model Prisa declared that it had some 45,000 subscribers), and, on the other, embracing the payment model meant diminishing the presence and social influence of the newspaper in a market of traditional and new players still in the process of being configured.

Thus, for example, during the hours following the Madrid 11-M terrorist attacks and due to the growing number of queries coming from all corners of the world, Prisa decided to cut *ElPaís.es*'s homepage in half, including only information about the attacks, increase bandwidth to respond to requests for information, and open the website pages. As we pointed out elsewhere: "By making the contents of the online newspaper available to any reader (and not only to those customers who had paid for their subscriptions), its managers chose not to sacrifice their presence and influence on news flows for the sake of the payment model" (Albornoz, 2007: 256).

However, the fleeting incursion of the online version of *El País* into the payment model meant a serious setback for Prisa, which took time to regain the leadership of digital newspapers. Almost two decades after that failed attempt to monetize the online presence of Grupo Prisa's main news media, its managers planned the return to the payment model in a staggered manner, reinforcing, first of all, the subscription model. To this end, in September 2018 Prisa signed an agreement with The Washington Post Company, owned by Amazon, to incorporate the Arc Publishing content manager with which the US newspaper works. Once implemented, this technological platform would make it possible to implement the payment wall at the levels decided by the newspaper's management and commercial department. In March 2020, *El País* announced that it was embracing the subscription model for its digital version following the footsteps of *The New York Times* (US), *The Washington Post* (US), *Financial Times* (UK), *Le Monde* (France), *The Guardian* (UK), *The Wall Street Journal* (US) and *Corriere della Sera* (Italy). Among the different digital subscription models that exist, *El País* opts for the so-called porous one: readers will be able to access 10 articles a month for free. At the same time, it is still necessary to register, free of charge, for some articles. Current subscribers to the print edition will have access to the digital edition at no additional cost (EL PAÍS, 2020).

At the international level, it should be noted that on November 26, 2013, the publisher of *El País* launched its online edition in Portuguese – the first in a language other than Spanish – for the Brazilian public. The progress of this edition coordinated from São Paulo is remarkable: in its first four years of existence, it was positioned among the six most read newspapers in this South American country (EL PAÍS, 2017b).

Months after the publication of the letter that in 2016 then director of *El País* Antonio Caño addressed to his editorial staff, foreseeing the disappearance of the printed edition, the newspaper's own pages announced that "*El País* registers more than 100 million monthly unique visitors", consolidating its leadership among the information media in Spanish and Portuguese, and placing itself at the bottom of the top ten most read newspapers in the world (see Table 5.1). Of the 100.3 million users reached in October 2017, half were outside Spain, especially in Latin America (EL PAÍS, 2017b). All figures of

Table 5.1 World's Top Ten Most Read Online News Outlets, 2017

Rank	Domain	Headquarters
1	xinhuanet.com	Beijing, China
2	nytimes.com	New York, US
3	people.com.cn	Beijing, China
4	theguardian.com	London, UK
5	dailymail.co.uk	London, UK
6	washingtonpost.com	Washington, US
7	telegraph.co.uk	London, UK
8	express.co.uk	London, UK
9	independent.co.uk	London, UK
10	elpais.com	Madrid, Spain

Source: Ranking elaborated by the publisher of *El País* from ComScore data

online readership must, however, be considered very carefully because of the very different and controversial ways of measuring readers on the Internet, including *El País* dropping from some historical media audits when losing its leadership in them.

In 2020, *El País* kept four online editions of the newspaper: Spain, America, Brazil, and *elpais.cat* – the Catalan edition of the newspaper. These editions are fed both by the company's offices in Madrid, Barcelona, Mexico City, Washington, and São Paulo, and by an important – though declining – network of correspondents and collaborators around the world.

Faced with this presence on the digital terrain, the circulation of the printed edition outside Spain is gradually becoming extinct. For example, since mid-2018, *El País* has been online-only in Chile, the Dominican Republic, and Miami, Florida – markets in which the newspaper was printed in collaboration with local media. However, it was decided to keep the printed edition for Mexico, Argentina, and Peru (EL PAÍS, 2018b).

According to a May 2018 estimate, made with metrics from Grupo Prisa's own press publisher, *El País* claimed to be the world's leading Spanish-language media, with 65 million readers if its web and print editions are combined. And it pointed out as key data demonstrating the newspaper's internationalization that 43 per cent of visits to the web editions came from Latin American countries. In addition, the press release published by *El País* (EL PAÍS, 2018b) stated that:

> Virtual support broadens the reading experience with extra content such as videos, photo galleries, podcasts, etc. that enrich the articles and reports. In this sense, *El País* is working on the development of

Cultural Profile 95

new narratives, multimedia specials and projects such as El País_LAB, which promotes avant-garde digital content. However, given that the printed version is important for many readers, it is available for download in countries where there is no printed edition through the Kiosko y Más platform, which can be accessed from a mobile phone, tablet, PC or laptop, and where all the newspaper's magazine offerings are available: *El País Semanal*, *Icon*, *SModa*, *Buenavida*, and *Retina*.

In autumn 2019, Grupo Prisa declared that *El País* had 59.8 million unique users per month worldwide (PC + mobile worldwide), with 48 per cent of these users coming from outside Spain. Users from Latin American countries (80 per cent) and the United States (11 per cent) accounted for most of this traffic generated outside the Spanish market. In addition, the newspaper had 23 million followers on the main social networks – Facebook, Twitter, Instagram, and YouTube – with 78 million video replays on average monthly.[10]

Cadena SER: The Talk Radio of Reference for Spaniards

Cadena SER has been the leading audience network of Spanish radio for over a quarter of a century, comfortably surpassing the offerings of other general radio stations such as Cadena COPE (an acronym for Cadena de Ondas Populares Españolas, formerly called Radio Popular, owned by the Spanish Episcopal Conference's company Radio Popular S.A.), Onda Cero (currently belonging to the radio group Atresmedia Radio, owned by Atresmedia Corporación), and RNE (Radio Nacional de España, Spain's national public radio service).

In 1992, the year in which Grupo Prisa took absolute control of Cadena SER, it had a daily audience of approximately 2.68 million listeners, in a territory of just over 39 million inhabitants (Figure 5.2). After that, the number of listeners of Prisa's talk radio began to grow year after year, reaching 4.15 million listeners in 1996. That was the year of the close general election between Felipe González (PSOE) and José María Aznar (PP), which ended up ousting the socialist leader from the government after 14 years in office.

Since then, with the exception of the 1998–1999 biennium, Cadena SER has had more than four million listeners a year, in a territory that by 2010 had a population of approximately 47 million people. It should be noted that the sustained growth in the number of listeners of Cadena SER between 1998 and 2004 was related to the fact that during that period, the Prisa radio network was the only one to hold a critical voice against the Aznar government (1996–2004). The figure of Iñaki Gabilondo at the head of the morning news program *Hoy por hoy* was an outstanding reference then. Thus, Grupo Prisa's radio established a solitary and clear opposition to COPE, Onda Cero, and RNE, radio networks that provided news coverage in line with the government's interests.

So far this century, 2004's spectacular rise in audience numbers, the year of the 11-M attacks in Madrid, stands out. The greatest increase in the number of listeners was related to the role played by Cadena SER during the days following this tragic event, which served, as we commented earlier, to dismantle the government's version of the possible responsibility for the attacks. The protagonism of Cadena SER took place through both the airwaves and its website, where it was possible to follow the live broadcast of the programming – there were 750,000 player openings and visits to informative content, and around three million page views daily between March 11 and 14 (Doval Avendaño, 2010).

According to the General Media Survey (or EGM, for Estudio General de Medios),[11] Cadena SER's accumulated daily audience during 2019 was approximately 4.15 million listeners. This figure was 1.02 million more listeners than that obtained by COPE, the second talk radio network; almost 2.32 million listeners more than Onda Cero; and 2.97 million more listeners than RNE (EGM, 3rd wave 2019).

Cadena SER's leadership in 2019 could be seen from Monday to Sunday and in all time slots. The morning program *Hoy por hoy*, which runs for more than six hours from Monday to Friday, continued to be the most-listened-to radio program in Spain with currently 2.81 million listeners per day (EGM, 3rd wave 2019). It is a leadership that has remained uninterrupted for more than a decade (11 years and 35 waves of the EGM). Regarding the programming of the rest of the broadcasters competing for audience, it should be noted that *Hoy por hoy* exhibited 585,000 listeners more than *Herrera en la COPE* (COPE) and more than 1.64 million with respect to *Más de uno* (Onda Cero).

Cadena SER's other emblematic news program, *Hora 25*, maintained its uninterrupted leadership for eight years. In 2019 it was followed on weekdays by almost one million listeners. The radio programs that compete with this informative analysis program, *La linterna* (COPE), *La brújula* (Onda Cero), and *24 horas* (RNE), had 872,000, 372,000, and 315,000 listeners, respectively.

Finally, apart from the absolute dominance of Cadena SER in the field of talk radio, it should be noted that the main music stations of Grupo Prisa are well received by the Spanish audience. Los 40 dominates music radio with nearly 2.84 million listeners daily. This radio network was the second most listened to in Spain, behind Cadena SER, in 2019. Behind Los 40 was Cadena Dial, which harvested approximately 2.11 million listeners daily in 2019 (EGM, 3rd wave 2019).

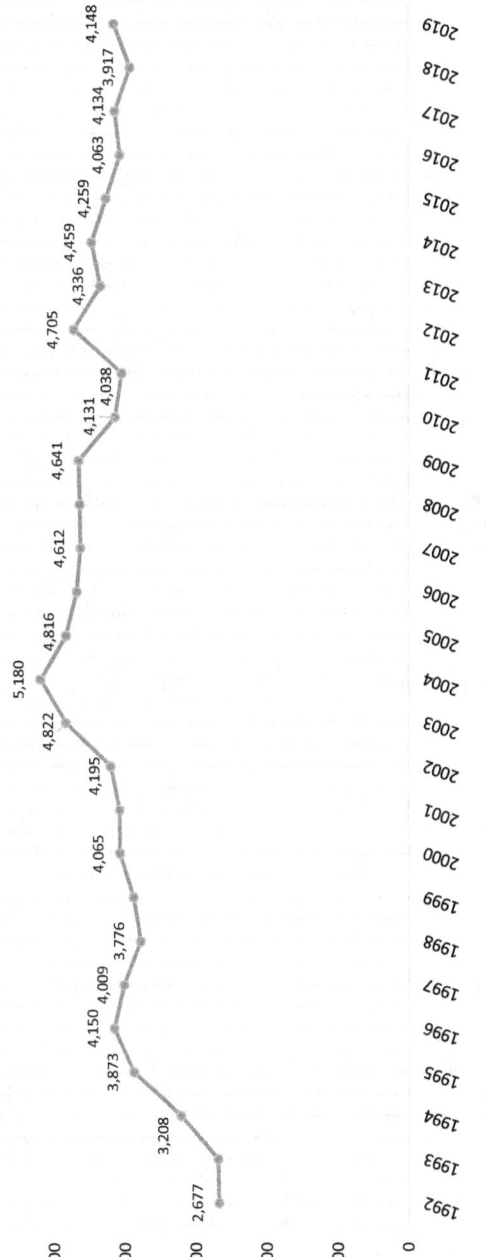

Figure 5.2 Cadena SER: Daily Audience Between 1992 and 2019 (Expressed in Thousands of Listeners)

Source: EGM (AIMC, 1993–2019)

Note: Cumulative audience, Monday through Sunday, total generalist radio, 3rd wave, February–November, Estudio General de Medios (EGM)

Notes

1. At the time of joining Grupo Prisa, Santillana was the world's leading Spanish-language publishing group. It specialized in educational books, but was also present in general publishing through publishers such as Aguilar, Alfaguara, Altea, Taurus, and Richmond Publishing.
2. In its 44-year history, the newspaper has had six editors: Juan Luis Cebrián (1976–1988), Joaquín Estefanía (1988–1993), Jesús Ceberio (1993–2006), Javier Moreno (2006–2014), Antonio Caño (2014–2018), and Soledad Gallego-Díaz (2018–).
3. Carlos Barreda points out that, in the last years of Franco's regime, Cadena SER "was bolder and was able to circumvent, with a certain amount of consent and tolerance from the authorities, the monopoly held by Radio Nacional on political information. As early as 1962, it began broadcasting an information magazine called 'Matinal'. . . . Another spearhead was the news programme 'Hora 25', which began broadcasting in 1972. Despite its untimely broadcasting time, it soon acquired great prestige" (Barrera, 1995: 168–169).
4. In 2018, after the removal of Hernández-Rodicio (now head of the Events department of Grupo Prisa), the management of Cadena SER was assumed by Daniel Gavela, a historical journalist of the house, who was director of Cadena SER (1994–2001) and later general director of Cadena SER-Unión Radio (2001–2006), with direct responsibility in the content area.
5. See Escolar 2016.
6. Interview with Ignacio Escolar on public television in the Basque Country, "Existe el periodismo independiente?" on *Sin ir más lejos (SIML)*, an ETB–2 opinion and debate program, April 28, 2016, www.eitb.eus/es/television/programas/sin-ir-mas-lejos/videos/detalle/4025950/video-ignacio-escolar-no-me-podia-callar-lo-cebrian/.
7. On December 18, 2004, more than 74 personalities from the literary world – Mario Vargas Llosa, Rafael Sánchez Ferlosio, Juan Marsé, and Eduardo Mendoza, among others – signed a letter addressed to the newspaper's management expressing their concern "for the damage suffered by the newspaper's credit" and "for the possibility of future criticism in the pages of *El País*".
8. With regard to integrated learning systems, in mid-2019 Manuel Mirat stated: "[before] investors could not find other similar companies to compare [Santillana] with. That has changed and there is a similar smaller company that came out a year ago on the NASDAQ: Arco. It is only present in the Brazilian market. Its stock market value is more than 1.9 billion dollars" (Jiménez and Delgado, 2019a).
9. *El País*, together with the evening newspaper *Diario 16*, the Catalanist *Avui* (Barcelona 1976–2011; in Catalan, it was the result of popular capitalization; today converted into *El Punt Avui*), the Basque nationalist *Deia* (Bilbao, 1977–), and the radical *Egin* (Hernani, 1977–1998) – the latter two with partial use of the Basque language – symbolize the political change that has taken place since the death of the dictator Franco (Guillamet, 2018: 11–12).
10. Information provided by Grupo Prisa through its institutional website (October 2019), www.prisa.com/es/info/el-pais.
11. The EGM is a study on media consumption in Spain carried out by the Association for Media Research (in Spanish, Asociación para la Investigación de Medios de Comunicación, AIMC). The methodology consists of personal interviews in the homes of the 30,000 people surveyed in the multimedia survey. To

this sample are added monomedia sample extensions for some particular media (radio, press, magazines, television), which are carried out, in most cases, by telephone survey.

Bibliography

Albornoz, L.A. (2007). *Periodismo digital. Los grandes diarios en la Red*. Buenos Aires: La Crujía.

APM (Asociación de Prensa de Madrid) (2016). *Comunicado de la APM en el Día Mundial de la Libertad de Prensa*. Madrid: APM, May 2.

Barrera, C. (1995). *Periodismo y franquismo: De la censura a la apertura*. Barcelona: Ediciones Internacionales Universitarias.

Caño, A. (2016). "Carta abierta del director de *El País* a la Redacción del periódico," *El País*, March 3.

Casqueiro, J. (2018). "La fabulosa historia de la Constitución y de la democracia contada para niños," *El País*, November 24.

C.L.B. (2015). "*The New York Times* acusa a *El País* de 'usar sus páginas para llevar a cabo una 'vendetta' corporativa'," *ElPlural.com*, November 13.

CNMC (National Commission for Markets and Competition, Spain) (2019). *La CNMC multa a 34 editoriales de libros de texto no universitarios y a la asociación ANELE por crear un mecanismo para restringir políticas y condiciones comerciales*. Madrid: CNMC, May 31.

DIRCONFIDENCIAL (2017). "El País renuncia a buena parte de sus ingresos al quitar los anuncios de contactos," *Dirconfidencial*, July 22.

Doval Avendaño, M. (2010). "Fuentes de información durante los tres días de marzo (11M al 13M) en los medios sociales españoles," Revista Latina de Comunicación Social, 65: 325–339.

EL PAÍS (1981). "*El País* con la Constitución," *El País*, February 24.

———. (1982). "*El País*, primer periódico español por su difusión," *El País*, February 17.

———. (1999). "*El País* batió su récord de difusión en 1998 con una media de 450.175 ejemplares diarios," *El País*, January 24.

———. (2005). "ElPais.es para todos," *El País*, June 3.

———. (2015). "Los editores responden a las acusaciones de *The New York Times*," *El País*, November 12.

———. (2017a). "En un mundo de ruido, una pregunta," *El País*, January 27.

———. (2017b). "*El País* registers more than 100 million monthly unique visitors," *El País*, November 8.

———. (2017c). "Cuarenta años de democracia y la mirada puesta en el futuro," *El País*, November 21.

———. (2017d). "Encuesta. ¿Se deben prohibir los toros?" *El País*, September 15.

———. (2018a). "*El País* crea una corresponsalía de género," *El País*, May 12.

———. (2018b). "*El País* alcanza los 65 millones de lectores," *El País*, July 26.

———. (2020). "*El País* lanza su suscripción digital," *El País*, March 5.

Enríquez Fuente, E. (2008). *El comercio de libros entre España y América latina: disonancia en la reciprocidad*. Alianza Internacional de Editores Independientes. https://www.alliance-editeurs.org/IMG/pdf/Comercio_del_libro.pdf

Escolar, I. (2016). "Juan Luis Cebrián me despide de la SER," *eldiario.es*, April 27.

Espantaleón Peralta, A. (2002). *El País y la transición política*. Granada: Universidad de Granada/Caja General de Ahorros de Granada.

Gálvez, J. (2014). "PRISA completa el 'entierro' de *El País* 'original': Sol Gallego-Díaz y Joaquín Estefanía separados del Consejo Editorial," *El Plural*, November 14.

Gaviña, S. (2009). "Crisol escribe su epílogo y cierra sus últimas tres librerías," *ABC*, April 30.

Granados Arocha, I./PODER (2019). "El negocio de los libros de educación en México," *El Espectador*, August 21.

Grassa Toro, C. (2018). *La fabulosa historia de nuestra democracia*. Madrid: Santillana.

Guillamet, J. (Ed.). (2018). *La transición de la prensa. El comportamiento político de diarios y periodistas*. Valencia: Universitat de València, pp. 9–15.

Imbert, G. and Vidal Beneyto, J. (1986). *El País o la referencia dominante*. Madrid: Editorial Mitre.

Jiménez, M. and Delgado, C. (2019a). "Manuel Mirat (Prisa/El País): 'La sociedad necesita buen periodismo y educación de calidad'," *El País*, June 2.

———. (2019b). "Miguel Ángel Cayuela (Santillana): 'Los sistemas de aprendizaje son el futuro de la educación'," *El País*, July 19.

Manrique Sabogal, W. (2016). "Las exportaciones de libros amortiguan la caída del sector," *El País*, May 27.

Mars, A. and Martínez Ahrens, J. (2015). "Los problemas económicos limitan la expansión de *The New York Times*," *El País*, November 12.

Minder, R. (2015). "Spain's News Media Are Squeezed by Government and Debt," *The New York Times*, November 5.

OCP (Observatory of Cultural Policies, Chile) (2012). *Estudio sobre las condiciones de internacionalización del libro chileno*. Santiago de Chile: OPC, National Council for Culture and the Arts, Government of Chile.

PRISA (2014). *Santillana vende sus Ediciones Generales a Penguin Random House para enfocarse en el área educativa*, Madrid: PRISA, March 2.

PÚBLICO/AGENCIAS (2018). "La redacción de *El País* respalda de forma masiva a Soledad Gallego-Díaz como directora con el 97,2% de los votos a favor," *Público*, June 7.

Savater, F. (2011). *Tauroética*. Madrid: Ediciones Turpial.

Schubert, A. (2002). *A las cinco de la tarde: Historia social del toreo*. Madrid: Turner Publicaciones.

Seoane, M.C. and Sueiro, S. (2004). *Una historia de El País y del Grupo Prisa*. Barcelona: Plaza & Janés.

Soteras, J. (2015). "*El País* cancela de forma 'definitiva' la publicación del suplemento de *The New York Times*," *InfoLibre*, November 12.

Soto Ivars, J. (2016). "Por qué llamé tirano a Cebrián en su propia casa," *El Confidencial*, May 31.

Thompson, J.B. (1995). *The Media and Modernity: A Social Theory of the Media*. London: Polity Press.

Ugalde, R. (2016). "DLJ pone en venta Santillana tras embolsarse cerca de 100 millones en dividendos," *El Confidencial*, January 25.

Urchaga Litago, J.D., Carballa Rivas, N.M. and García González, A. (2017). "Cobertura mediática de la prohibición de las corridas de toros en Cataluña a través de un análisis multivariante hj-biplot," *Prisma Social*, 19, 450–470.

Yárnoz, C. (2019). "Toros en cultura," *El País*, June 9.

Zarzalejos, A.G. (2018). "Prisa mira al pasado para afrontar su futuro en la era pos-Cebrián," *El Confidencial*, June 6.

6 Conclusion

Grupo Prisa has come a long way since it was founded in 1972, thanks to the initiative of José Ortega Spottorno, with the aim of publishing a newspaper that would break with the intellectual, technical, and professional hardship in which the Spanish press found itself at that time. *El País* was precisely the information outlet that best connected with a Spain that, after the death of Franco and the partial collapse of his regime, was taking its first steps into the path of the most advanced European democracies.

Fifteen years after the birth of *El País*, a newspaper that already enjoyed influence and prestige in Spain and abroad, it boasted within its pages of displaying the profile of the multimedia group it wanted to become. This was at the time when its then president, Jesús Polanco, was convinced that the company's European expansion would be established based on its strong position in the Spanish market. Polanco told the general meeting of shareholders:

> After the consolidation of *El País* and [Cadena] SER as leaders of the Spanish press and radio broadcasting, Prisa's objective is to build a communications group with a European projection that will develop the professional project launched 15 years ago with the publication of the newspaper *El País*.
>
> (PRISA, 1991)

Thinking about the configuration of the media scenario of the new millennium to come, he explained his conviction: "It is not possible that by then the current atomization of the press will continue, nor will the absurd system of television in Spain be sustained, while at the same time the European audiovisual scenario will change profoundly" (PRISA, 1991). Specifically, this pronouncement was made at a time when Prisa had set up the pay-TV signal Canal+ Spain – along with the French group Canal+, a company that was already present in Germany and Belgium – and was making incursions into film production and the management of audio-visual rights.

However, as we have seen throughout this volume, Prisa's accelerated international expansion did not focus on European territory but, rather, on Spanish- and Portuguese-speaking Latin American countries. Moreover, it was precisely the incursions into the field of television that made Prisa's own survival falter, as it was a means to contract an exorbitant economic debt in a very short period. The unfortunate takeover bid on 100 per cent of its subsidiary Sogecable, which sought to consolidate all of the company's businesses into a single enterprise, implied short-term loans that were to be renegotiated at the height of a global economic crisis.

Why Latin America? The orientation of Prisa's international expansion towards Latin America can be explained in terms of a cultural proximity founded on a three-centuries-old colonial past. That colonial past had led to the disappearance of entire communities and the plundering of the region's wealth, and, in turn, resulted in a more or less culturally and linguistically homogeneous region. The linguistic fact – Spanish and Portuguese are the two dominant languages – has been a major factor in both the spread of Prisa's flagship medium, *El País*, and the expansion of Santillana. Prisa's media have expanded in a region that traditionally suffers from the absence of public broadcasting services, reports low newspaper readership rates (like Spain), and has media outlets that provide little coverage of international affairs.

On the other hand, we should remember that the advance towards Latin America by Grupo Prisa is not an isolated one, but rather a movement that takes place within the framework of the expansion of numerous Spanish companies. The neoliberal reforms of the 1990s undertaken by numerous Latin American countries based on the Washington Consensus[1] favoured this type of action. The presence of companies in key sectors in Latin American countries – telecommunications (Telefonica), electricity (Endesa), banking (Banco Santander, BBVA), and hydrocarbons (Repsol) – turned Spain into the second leading country in direct investment in the region, only behind the United States, and numerous analysts denounced a second Spanish colonization.[2]

The presence of Grupo Prisa outlets in Latin American countries gave rise to numerous accusations of alignment with the interests of Spanish companies present in that region. In addition, there has been criticism about playing against self-proclaimed leftist or progressive political parties, social movements, and leaders who have come into power since the first decade of the new century.[3]

Outside the Market's Law

The death of its founder Jesús Polanco in 2007 – the year in which Prisa declared a record operating profit of 520 million euros – left the company in the hands of Juan Luis Cebrián on the eve of the great global economic crisis, which particularly affected Spain. According to several media analysts, Cebrián presided over an unprecedented collapse of a major European media company over the next decade. Prisa suffered a 99 per cent drop in its stock market value. And the generation of unpayable financial debt led the company to engage in a series of divestments and sales that culminated in the loss of power of the company's historic shareholders.

In any case, the acute crisis that still affects Grupo Prisa and its outlets (*El País*, Cadena SER, *As*, Cadena Dial, etc.) makes it an interesting case study. How and why did a media conglomerate that quickly accumulated a net bank debt of more than 5 billion euros in 2008 survive?

Perhaps it's easier to answer how this happened. The pages of this volume give an account of different processes that Prisa's managers followed to avoid declaring bankruptcy. They pursued, that is, on the one hand, a process of divestment from assets considered non-strategic, both in Spain and abroad. This divestment process, which affected Prisa's various business units, was accompanied by successive staff layoffs, voluntary redundancies, and reductions in workers' wages.

On the other hand, Prisa underwent complicated processes of debt renegotiation and capital increases, which included the conversion of part of the debt into shares. This led to the arrival of bankers and investment fund managers on Prisa's board of directors. We should note, however, that this was not a phenomenon particular to Prisa. The most important conglomerates operating in the Spanish market – owners of traditional media – have been co-opted by the banks. Grupo Vocento (*ABC*) enjoys a very close relationship with Banco Santander; Grupo Godó (*La Vanguardia*, RAC1, 8tv) maintains a relationship with Caixabank that "could almost be considered a cold merger" (Rusiñol, 2016: 34); RCS MediaGroup, owner of Unidad Editorial (*El Mundo*, *Expansión*, *Marca*), is supported by the Italian bank Mediobanca; and Grupo Planeta (Antena 3, La Sexta, *La Razón*, Onda Cero) maintains a close relationship with Banco Sabadell. This is clearly a delicate situation that puts freedom of expression at risk and, consequently, threatens the quality of Spanish democracy.[4]

Finally, it is worth noting the support of the Spanish government at the time in exchange for benevolent or at least non-contentious journalistic coverage. The Spanish media reported that the vice president of the government of Mariano Rajoy (PP), the lawyer Soraya Sáenz de Santamaría, was key in the approval of Prisa's debt refinancing plan that took place at the end of 2013, and in which 28 banks and 17 investment funds took part (Arranz, 2015; Jiménez, 2019: 48). It has also been reported that this same powerful government figure was the one who prevented Juan Luis Cebrián from being replaced at the head of the company because she did not like the profile of the proposed replacement (Cano, 2017).

The question of why Prisa has survived its most acute economic crisis in its more than four decades of existence prompts several theories. It cannot be forgotten that Prisa is a media conglomerate with an international projection – limited mainly to the Spanish- and Portuguese-speaking countries of Latin America – that owns the general information newspaper and the most heard talk and music radio networks in its home market. Nor can we forget that, like other Spanish media conglomerates, Prisa is part of the country's establishment. Over the years, Prisa has become a sort of public relations powerhouse that permeates the different segments of Spanish society (politics, culture, education, sports, etc.) and has a special penetration in the Latin American region. It is common, for example, for Latin American presidential candidates and elected presidents to hold meetings with Prisa executives and give exclusive interviews to *El País*.

As we have seen in the previous pages, an important part of the work carried out by Grupo Prisa in the field of public relations takes place through the organization of awards and events both inside and outside Spain. One example is "*El País* con tu futuro", an event co-organized by the newspaper's publisher and the Fundación Santillana, which aims to put young people between the ages of 16 and 18 in contact with professionals from different fields to guide them in their career choice. The fifth instance of this event, held in December 2019, was sponsored by Banco Santander, Telefónica, and Google; it also received support from Airbus, Bayer, the Colegio Universitario de Estudios Financieros (a private Spanish university specializing in banking and finance), and the University of Castilla-La Mancha.

On the other hand, there is Santillana, a group of companies and a wide range of products (school texts, language books, digital learning systems) that maintain a strong presence in the educational field both in Spain and in 21 other countries. As noted earlier, Santillana is considered "the jewel in the crown" of Prisa because it generates approximately half of its income and more than 60 per cent of its gross operating profit.

Thus, we might consider that the disappearance of the most powerful and internationalized communication-education group in contemporary Spain would have affected not only its managers and workers, but a wider set of stakeholders, including powerful figures of the political and economic sphere. Would there be any interest in saving a company that had reached the economic, political, bureaucratic, academic, and cultural elite not only of Spain but also of the Spanish- and Portuguese-speaking countries? Business weakness, in any case, often goes hand in hand with docility (or information blackout and status quo alignment).

In his analysis of the Spanish media, the journalist Pere Rusiñol (2016: 36), founding partner of the magazine *Alternativas Económicas* and former employee of *El País*, points out:

> The global financial crash put an end to the party, and the media groups, up to their eyeballs in debt and without a euro in cash, were unable to

repay the loans. If they had made pens, they would most likely be closed today. But they manufacture the agenda and the information from which citizens make their decisions: the creditor banks agreed to turn overdue loans into shares. In the emblematic case of Prisa, three of the four banks that made up the pool that had financed Sogecable's controversial takeover bid – Banco Santander, Caixabank, and HSBC; only Bankia was left out – agreed to swap part of the debt for shares in the group in 2012, and they took almost 25% of the company.

Apart from the expulsion of the traditional managers (Polanco's family and Juan Luis Cebrián), one of the main and evident consequences of the severe process of divestment and debt renegotiation faced by Grupo Prisa has been the reduction of its financial debt, which went from 5.135 billion euros to 1.351 billion euros between 2008 and 2018. Such a steep decrease in debt allows market analysts to assert that the worst is over. However, Prisa's survival has led to the global devaluation of the company, the lessening of international presence (we write these lines when Prisa has taken various attempts to exit the Portuguese audio-visual market and announced its intention to leave the publishing company that issues *Le Monde*, and a severe crisis of legitimacy that affected, and still affects, its media).

The company's loss in value has been evident in the exit of Grupo Prisa from the IBEX 35 and by the steep and rapid depreciation in value of the company's shares, which fell from 5.90 euros in 2016 to 2.05 euros in 2017 (-65 per cent within an eight-month period).

Above all, Prisa's media, and especially its flagship publication, *El País*, have not been unscathed by the rescue operation of financial capital. In its much-commented "turn to the right" led by Juan Luis Cebrián and Antonio Caño, *El País* has not been able to recruit conservative readers, who have at their disposal a variety of options in the Spanish news market (*ABC, El Mundo, La Razón*, and other digital publications), while at the same time disenchanting some of the readers who identify with more progressive social positions. On the other hand, the change in the editorial line of the once "dominant reference" in Spain (Imbert and Vidal Beneyto, 1986), together with the expulsion of journalists and historical collaborators from this newspaper, has given rise to the emergence of other journalistic media that have clearly positioned themselves to the left and have embraced values such as democracy, transparency, and ethics. Such is the case of the digital dailies *eldiario.es, infoLibre*, and the monthly magazine *Alternativas Económicas*.[5]

The Future Isn't What it Used to Be . . .

The passing of time will dictate whether Grupo Prisa has begun a new stage in its history with the coming of new executives (Manuel Mirat, CEO; Javier

Monzón, non-executive chairman; Joseph Oughourlian, non-executive vice-chairman) and a board of directors dotted with independent members, which has been labelled in the media as "the most professional and least political board in the history of Prisa" (Cano, 2019). Similarly, it remains to be seen if that means it is also the least financialized board. In addition, Prisa's media management has appointed professionals who are part of the company's history (Soledad Gallego-Díaz, Daniel Gavela, and Vicent Argudo at the head of *El País*, Cadena SER, and the music radio network, respectively).

The challenges currently faced by Grupo Prisa, focused on reducing its remaining debt and on strengthening its media and educational segment, are of enormous importance. How to maintain and increase the company's social importance through the formulation of public agendas, how to continue the digital transformation of the various units, and how to generate income linked to the presence of products and services in the digital environment are some of the most significant questions.

In this sense, Prisa no longer expresses its desire to become a communications group with European reach, nor does it have in mind a commitment to be one of the leaders of the audio-visual market (something that Telefónica has achieved in the Spanish market). On the contrary, the company's executives have expressed their intention to continue along the path of austerity of recent years and to concentrate on expressing the maximum potential of the company's different lines of business (Fernández, 2018).

In the education segment, the goal is to continue the digital transformation from traditional textbooks through comprehensive educational solutions, strengthen the product offering by focusing on quality, and improve efficiencies and cost control. There has even been speculation in the press that Prisa is researching how to promote so-called learning systems, considering the possibility of segregating the Internet-based education division, the fastest growing business within Santillana, in order to take it to the stock market.[6]

Regarding its radio business, we must point out that Prisa Radio is one of the largest Spanish-speaking radio groups with approximately 23 million listeners and more than 1,000 stations, including its owned-and-operated and affiliate stations, and is distributed in 13 countries. The strategic focus in this segment is on maintaining leadership, deepening the digital transformation from an analogue model to one of digital multimedia content, and strengthening the product portfolio through the expansion of its global brands, such as Los 40, and the development of the first podcast platform, Podium Podcast, for Spanish-speaking countries.

With respect to the press sector, a competitive market in full digital transformation where the traditional headlines suffer from the exodus of advertising investments towards Google and Facebook, Prisa maintains *El País* as its flagship publication. Although the circulation figures are constantly dropping, *ElPais.com* reports to be the number one portal in the world for

Conclusion

information in Spanish, with 84 million unique browsers, half of which are in Spain and half abroad, most of them in Latin America (Gallego-Díaz, 2019). In this context, Prisa maintains that it is increasingly important to "respond with a quality product, offer new services and specialized multimedia content, develop distribution alliances, internationalize brands, implement mixed business models (free/pay), and innovate in advertising formats" (Fernández, 2018).

The example to follow is that of *The New York Times*, which has found a profitable model that combines advertising, subscriptions, and event revenues. To this end, the Prisa newspaper publisher has signed an agreement with The Washington Post Company to implement the Arc Publishing content manager in *El País* and is finalizing the details for implementing a subscription-based payment system (paywall). There is also an expansion project underway in Latin America (which will include hiring journalists), and another project to develop *El País*'s cultural supplement, Babelia, which will be identical in Spanish for Spain and Latin America (Gallego-Díaz, 2019).

Grupo Prisa tackles the third decade of the twenty-first century in the hands of banks and non-Spanish institutional investors (Amber Capital, Mexican entrepreneurs and banks, and international investment funds own more than 50 per cent of the shares) and with a majority of its income coming from outside its home market. While on the economic front the immediate goal is to make the company's financial structure more efficient and improve its debt levels, on the strategic front, Prisa aims to provide its outlets with credibility and quality educational content.

While the future is no longer what it used to be … it has yet to be written.

Notes

1. The term Washington Consensus was coined in 1989 by economist John Williamson. His aim was to describe a set of ten relatively specific formulas, which he considered to constitute the "standard" reform package for developing countries hit by crisis, according to the institutions under the orbit of Washington, DC, such as the International Monetary Fund (IMF), the World Bank, and the US Department of the Treasury. The formulas included policies that advocated macroeconomic stabilization, economic liberalization with respect to both trade and investment, reduction of the state, and expansion of market forces within the domestic economy.
2. According to Pedro Ramiro and Alejandro Pulido (2009: 21): "All this expansion of Spanish multinationals has taken place in a very short time: barely a decade and a half. Spain, which in the 1980s only received foreign investment and had a minimal trade opening, became the country that invested most in Latin America at the end of the 1990s: in 1999, it concentrated 66% of its investments in this region and became the sixth largest investor in the world. Between 1993 and 2006, total Spanish Foreign Direct Investment (FDI) accumulated in Latin America amounted to more than 110 billion euros".
3. On this subject, see Ángel Badillo *et al.* 2015.

Conclusion 109

4. On this subject, see the functioning of the Spanish press described by the former director of the newspaper *El Mundo*, David Jiménez (2019).
5. Since 2012, the publisher Diario de Prensa Digital has been publishing *eldiario.es* and, every trimester, the monographic paper magazine of the same name. On the other hand, Ediciones Prensa Libre, in association with *Mediapart.fr* (a French paid digital newspaper directed by the former editor in chief of *Le Monde*, Edwy Plenel) and the publishing house Edhasa, has been publishing the digital daily *infoLibre* and the monthly paper magazine *Tinta Libre* since 2013. *Alternativas Económicas* (which was modelled on *Alternatives Economiques*, a French magazine published by a worker cooperative of journalists in France) was first published in April 2013. *Alternativas Económicas* is published monthly by the worker cooperative of Spanish journalists with the same name, Alternativas Económicas. The contributors are mostly journalists who previously worked for *El País*, *Público*, and *El Periódico de Catalunya*.
6. According to newspaper sources (EL CONFIDENCIAL, 2019), the operation was proposed by Goldman Sachs and Morgan Stanley, the investment banks that took the Brazilian company Arco Platform Ltd. to the stock market. Arco Platform was placed on the US NASDAQ in September 2018 at a price of 17.50 dollars per share and was trading at 46 dollars at the end of 2019, a 160% increase in value that boosted its capitalization to 2.4 billion dollars.

Bibliography

Arranz, R. (2015). "Cebrián echa una mano a Soraya Sáenz de Santamaría en un momento duro y le sitúa a la cabeza del PP," *VoxPópuli*, December 12.
Badillo, A., Mastrini, G. and Marenghi, P. (2015). "Teoría crítica, izquierda y políticas públicas de comunicación: el caso de América Latina y los gobiernos progresistas," *Comunicación y Sociedad* (new period), 24: 95–126.
Cano, F. (2017). "Soraya aborta el relevo de Cebrián para no perder el control de Prisa," *El Español*, October 14.
——— (2019). "Amber busca apoyos para que el consejo de Prisa cese a Monzón tras su imputación en la Púnica," *El Español*, September 4.
EL CONFIDENCIAL (2019). "Prisa planea vender o sacar a bolsa su división de educación por internet," *El Confidencial*, December 9.
Fernández, D. (2018). "PRISA abre una nueva etapa," *El País*, February 25.
Gallego-Díaz, S. (2019). *Presentation at the Foro de la Nueva Comunicación*. Madrid: PRISA, November 26.
Imbert, G. and Vidal Beneyto, J. (Eds.). (1986). *El País o la referencia dominante*. Barcelona: Editorial Mitre.
Jiménez, D. (2019). *El Director*. Madrid: Libros del K.O.
PRISA (1991). "Jesús Polanco: 'Nuestro objetivo es un grupo de comunicación con proyección europea," *El País*, June 21.
Ramiro, P. and Pulido, A. (2009). *Las multinacionales españolas y el negocio de la responsabilidad. Análisis de la Responsabilidad Social Corporativa de las empresas transnacionales en Colombia*. Bogota: Observatory of Multinationals in Latin America (OMAL).
Rusiñol, P. (2016). "La gran captura," in *eldiario.es*, 14 (monographic: El periodismo acosado [Harassed journalism]). Madrid: Diario de Prensa Digital, pp. 33–39.

Index

Note: Page numbers in *italics* indicate a *figure* and page numbers in **bold** indicate a **table** on the corresponding page.

3i Group plc 18, 20, **29**, 32
11-M terrorist attacks 53, 81, 93, 96; Al Qaeda 53, 81
23-F coup d'état (Spain) 10, 11 72, 73, 81; Tejerazo 10, 72

ABC (newspaper, Spain) 4, 53, 89, 90, 104, 106
Adar Capital Partners LTD (investor fund, Israel) 50
advertising investment crisis 39
Aguilar, Miguel Ángel (Prisa's journalist) 75, 76
Alandete, David (former *El País*' deputy director) 81
Alcántara Rojas, Roberto (Mexican businessmen) 41, **50**, 56, **58**
Alfonso XIII (King of Spain; 1886–1941) 4, 22n10
Alternativas Económicas (economic magazine, Spain) 105, 106, 109n5
Altice NV (telecommunications, Netherlands), sale of Media Capital to 21
Amber Capital (investment fund, UK) 9, **49**, **50**, 50, 56, **58**, 108
Antena 3 (free-to-air television channel, Spain) 104
Antena 3 de Televisión (television company, Spain) 14, 23n19
Antena 3 Radio (radio company, Spain) 13, 22n15, 23n16, **27**,
Arena, Juan (Spanish businessmen) 56

Argentina: Prisa Radio in 16, **28**, 32, 80; Prisa's employees in 62; Crisol bookstores in 86; Santillana in 32, 87; Grupo Norma in 23n23, 44n1; *El País* newspaper in 33, 94; Prisa's revenues from 36; Los 40 radio in 83
Argudo, Vicent (current Prisa's musical radio chief) 107
As (Prisa's sports newspaper) 6, 12, 32, 33; online international editions 30, **31**, 33, 45n5; As.com 17; Premios As del Deporte 66
Asensio, Antonio (Spanish media businessman; 1947–2001) 15, 23n19
ATB (private free-to-air tv, Bolivia) 13
Atresmedia (media holding, Spain) 22n15, 44, 45n10, 68n5, 87, 95
Audiovisual Sport – AVS (Spain) 15, 23n19
A vivir que son dos días (Cadena SER's radio program) 80
Avui (newspaper, Spain) 79, 98n9
Awards of Grupo Prisa: Premios 40 Principales América 66; Premios AS del Deporte 66; Premios Cinco Días a la Innovación Empresarial 67; Premios Dial 66; Premios Ondas 66; Premios Radiolé 67; WDM Radio Awards 67
Axel Springer SE (publisher, Germany) 39
Aznar, José María (former Spanish president; 1953–) 15, 18, 38, 52, 53, 67n3, 81, 95

Babelia (*El País*' cultural supplement) 86, 108
Banca March (bank, Spain) 48
Banco Bilbao Vizcaya Argentaria – BBVA (bank, Spain) 48, 103
Banco Santander (bank, Spain) **50**, 57, **58**, 103, 104, 105, 106; Grupo Santander 66
Bankinter (bank, Spain) 14, 48, 56
BBC Radio 5 Live (public radio station, UK) 80
Be Mad (private free-to-air tv, Spain) 5
Berggruen, Nicholas (Prisa's financial investor; 1961–) 56
Berlusconi, Silvio (former Italian prime minister; 1936–) 4, 18
Bertelsmann (multimedia conglomerate, Germany) 20, 86; purchase of Santillana Ediciones Generales 30
board of directors, of Grupo Prisa 3, 22n8, 38, 41, 47, 56, **58–59**, 65, 104, 107
Boing (private free-to-air tv, Spain) 5
Bolivian press, and Grupo Prisa 13
Borges, Jorge Luis (Argentinian writer; 1899–1986) 87
Bourdieu, Pierre (French sociologist; 1930–2002) 71
podcast, branded projects of Grupo Prisa 83–84
Brand Solutions see Prisa Brand Solutions
Brazil: Grupo Prisa in 6, **28**, **31**; *El País* in 8; Santillana in 32, 84, 86, 87; Media Capital in 34; Prisa's revenues from 36; Prisa's employees in 62; *El País* newspaper in 55, 84; Editora Moderna 16; Media Capital in 17
BuenaVida (*El País*' magazine) 32–33
bullfights/bullfighting events 78–79

Cabanillas Alonso, Pío (Spanish politician) 52
cable pay-TV 40
Cadena Dial (Prisa's radio network, Spain) 32, 66, 83, 96, 104
Cadena SER (Prisa's radio network, Spain) 11–12, 18–19, 22n10–11, **31**, 32, 53, 54, 72, 74, 76, 78, 79–84, 89, 95–97, 98n3–4, 102, 104, 107; acquisition of 13, 22n12, **27**; audience of *97*; availability of programs 83; political shift of 82–83; programs aired by 80; Radio Barcelona and 66; CadenaSER.com 17
Caixa Bank (bank, Spain) 3, 104
Caja Madrid (bank, Spain) 48
Calderón, Felipe (former Mexican president; 1962–2006) 55
Calvo-Sotelo, Leopoldo (former Spanish president; 1926–2008) 10, 22n6
Canal+ (pay-TV, Spain) 16, 23n18, **27**, **29**, 102; criticism of 14; revenues of 20; Plus.es 17
Canal+ France 14, 15, 102
Canal Satélite Digital - CSD (pay-TV, Spain) 14–16, 17, 18, 23n21, 38
Caño, Antonio (former *El País*' editor) 74–77, 81, 92, 93, 106
Car (Prisa's magazine, Spain) 33
Carlos, Juan José de (Prisa's founder) 9, **49**
Carrousell deportivo (Cadena SER's radio program) 80
Casa del Libro (bookstore chain, Spain) 86
Catalonia: ban on bullfighting in 79; political repression of 4; Catalan independentist challenge 54
Cayuela, Miguel Ángel (Santillana's CEO) 84, 88
Ceberio, Jesús (former *El País*' editor; 1946–) 53, 98n2
Cebrián, Juan Luis (former Prisa's CEO and president; 1944–) 3, 6, 9, 12, 17, 37, 39, 41, 48, 54, 56, 61, 75, 98n2; political connections of 51–52; departure of 77; at 2008 shareholders' general meeting 40; father 73; Cadena SER and 81; and Panama Papers 76; and Ignacio Escolar case 82; and leadership of Grupo Prisa 103–104, 106
Cebrián, Vicente (journalist, Spain; 1914–2010) 67n2
Cela, Camilo José (1989 Nobel Prize in Literature; 1916–2002) 11
Chávez, Hugo (former Venezuelan president; 1954–2013) 55

Chile: Prisa Radio in 16, **28**, **31**, 32; Santillana in 21, 32, 65, 85, 87; Grupo Norma in 23n23, 44n1; *El País* in 33, 55, 94; Prisa employees in 62; Los 40 in 83
Cidade FM (radio station, Portugal) 17, 34
Cinco Días (Prisa's business and finance newspaper) 12, **27**, 31, 32, 67; CincoDías.com 17
Cinemanía (Prisa's film magazine, Spain) 12
Ciudadanos (political party, Spain) 54, 68n7, 75
Clásica FM Radio (Spain) 83
Claves de la razón práctica (Prisa's magazine, Spain) 12, 32
Colombia: Prisa Radio in 6, 16, **27**, 32; and Grupo Caracol 23n24, **31**, 80, 81; Santillana in 66, 84, 85, 87; Grupo Norma in 23n23, 44n1; *El País* newspaper in 33, 55; Grupo Prisa's employees in 62; Los 40 in 83
Conaliteg – Comisión Nacional de Libros de Texto Gratuitos (Mexico) 85–86
contact advertisements in *El País* 78
COPE, Cadena (radio network, Spain) 95, 96
corporate social responsibility – CSR, and Grupo Prisa 63–67, 68n3
Corriere della Sera (newspaper, Italy) 5, 93
Cortés, Juan Antonio (Santillana's founder; 1925–1998) 84
Costa Rica: Prisa Radio in 16, **29**, 32; Los 40 in **83**
Crisol bookstores (Spain) 18, **29**, 86
cross-media expansion, of Grupo Prisa 9, 10, 11–18, 26, 34, 35
Crown, Spanish 47, 54, 75, 78
CSD see Canal Satélite Digital
Cuadernos para el diálogo (Prisa's magazine, Spain) 52
Cuatro (private free-to-air channel, Spain) 5, 14, 16, 17, 18, **27**, **28**, **29**, 39, 45n9; Cuatro.com 17
cultural power 71

dailymail.co.uk (online newspaper, UK) **94**
Dar Al Sharq Holding Group (Qatar) 30, **57**

debt of Grupo Prisa: reduction plan 18–20, 41–44, 103; financial debt 5, 16, 35, **35**, 37, **49**, 57, 104; impact of 3, 6, 8, 15, 103–107; cause 39, 41–44, 76
Diario 16 (newspaper, Spain) 90, 98n9
Digital+ (pay-TV company, Spain) 15–16, 22n7, **28**, **29**, **31**; creation of 14, 38; revenues of 40; shares sold to Telefónica 19, 20, 23n25, 41
digital content, monetizing of 19, 41
Digital First Media (US) 41
digital terrestrial television – DTT 18; 22n7, 83
Disney (cinema, US) 38
diversification strategy, Grupo Prisa and 12–13, **27**–**28**, 57, 74, 86
divestment, Grupo Prisa and 6, 8, 13, 15, 18–21, 27, **29**, 35, 37, 104, 106
Divinity (private free-to-air television channel, Spain) 5
DLJ South American Partners (private equity fund) 18, **29**, 87

Echevarría-Babelia case, in *El País* newspaper 86
Echevarría, Ignacio (former *El País'* literary critic; 1960–) 86
Ediciones Castillo (MacMillan Education company, Mexico) 86
Editora Moderna (publisher, Brazil) 16, 23n22, **28**, **31**
Editorial Católica (publisher, Spain) 89
education-publishing sector see Santillana
Efe (public news agency, Spain) 81
Egin (Basque newspaper, Spain) 98n6
El Alcázar (newspaper, Spain) 90
ElConfidencial.com (online newspaper, Spain) 82
El Correo (newspaper, Spain) 90
eldiario.es (online newspaper, Spain) 82, 106, 109n5
El Globo (former Prisa's magazine, Spain) 12
El gran musical (former Prisa's magazine, Spain) 12
El Huffington Post (*HuffPos*' Spanish version) 32
El larguero (Cadena SER's radio program) 80, 81

Index

El Mundo (newspaper, Spain) 5, 90, 92, 104, 106, 109n4
El Nuevo Día (newspaper, Bolivia) 13
El País (Prisa's newspaper) 2, 3, 6, 8, 12, 18, 19, **31**, 32–33, 37, 43, 54, 72–79, 89–95, 105; changes in editorial content 75–78, 106, 107; circulation of 33; and 23-F coup d'état 21n3, 72–73; defensor del lector of 10, 78, 79; early years of 9–10, 21n2, 26, 47, 102; newspaper sales 90, *91*; as an online media outlet 41, 92; as a paywalled service 17; profile of 74–75; profitability of 9, 35; and reporting on the Madrid terrorist attacks 52–53; and Spain 40-40 Forum 65, 68n12; online edition of 17, 41, 92–94, 107–108; ClasificadosElPais.com 17; revenues from 35; and Latin American governments 55; employees of 61; and Babelia-Echevarría case 86, 98n7
El País (Prisa's publishing house) 12
El Periódico de Catalunya (newspaper, Spain) 53, 79, 90, 109n5
El Sol (newspaper, Spain) 9
Energy (free-to-air television channel, Spain) 5
Escolar, Ignacio (Spanish journalist; 1975–) 76, 81–82, 98n6
Estefanía, Joaquín (former *El País* editor; 1951–) 75, 98n2
ETA – Euskadi Ta Askatasuna 53, 81
European Telecommunications Satellite Organization – EUTELSAT 57, 58
Expansión (economic and business newspaper, Spain) 5, 104
express.co.uk (online newspaper, UK) **94**
Extra (newspaper, Bolivia) 13

Facebook (US) 95, 107
Factoría de Ficción (private free-to-air television channel, Spain) 5
Falange Española de las JONS (Spain) 4, 67n2
Financial Times (newspaper, UK) 93
financialization 3; of Grupo Prisa 41–44
Fininvest (multimedia holding, Italy) 4
football broadcasting rights in Spain 15, 23n19, 23n20, 38, 40–41, 42, 54

Franco, Francisco (former Spanish dictator; 1892–1975) 6, 9, 51; death of 10, 50–51, 72, 98n9, 102; Francoism, victims of 51; Francoist oligarchy 5; Francoist regime 1, 2, 3, 4, 9, 10, 11, 51, 52; anti-Francoist opposition 12, 51; Francoist media 4, 22n13, 67n2, 98n3
Frankfurter Allgemeine Zeitung (newspaper, German) 61
Franklin, Martin E. (former Prisa's financial investor; 1964–) 56

Gabilondo, Iñaki (Spanish journalist; 1942–) 80, 95
Gallego-Díaz, Soledad (current *El País'* editor) 75, 77–78, 98n2, 107, 108
Garáfulic, Grupo (multimedia holding, Bolivia) 13, **27**, **29**
Gavela, Daniel (current Prisa Radio's CEO) 98n4, 107
Gestevisión Telecinco 14; Grupo Prisa deal with 18–19
global financial crisis 2, 43; global economic crisis 103; international economic crisis 8, 18; international capitalist crisis 9; global economic and financial crisis 28
GLR – Grupo Latino de Radio (Prisa Radio's company) 16 see Prisa Radio
Godó, Grupo (multimedia holding, Spain) 3, 4, 13, 20, **29**, 32, 104;
Godó, Javier (Spanish media businessman; 1941–) 4
Gol TV (private free-to-air television channel, Spain) 54
González, Felipe (former Spanish president; 1942–) 10, 14, 15, 22n12, 52, 74, 77, 95
Google (US) 105, 107
Gran Vía Musical – GVM (Prisa's musical unit, Spain) 13–14, **28**, 79
Grass, Günter (1999 Nobel Prize in Literature ;1927–2015) 87
Guardian, The (newspaper, UK) 74; theguardian.com 93–**94**
Guerra, Alfonso (Spanish politician; 1940–) 80
Guía del ocio (Prisa's magazine) 32

Index

Hernández-Rodicio, Antonio (current Prisa's head of events) 81, 98n4
Hora 25/Hora 25-Fin de semana (Cadena SER's radio program) 80, 96, 98n3
Hoy por hoy (Cadena SER's radio program) 80, 82, 95, 96
Hussein, Saddam (former Iraq's president; 1937–2006) 81

Iberoamericana Radio Chile (Prisa's radio subsidiary, Chile) 16, **28**
Icon (Prisa's magazine, Spain) 33, 95
Independent, The (newspaper, UK) 12, **27**; independent.co.uk **94**
infoLibre (online newspaper, Spain) 106
Instagram (US) 95
international organizations, Grupo Prisa support of 65–66
Iraq war 43, 67n3, 81; and Azores summit 67n3
Italy: Italian media companies 3; 4–5, 18, 39; Italian holding 104; press in 10, 74
ITT (telecommunications, US) 4
Izquierda Unida – IU (political party, Spain) 55

Jordán de Urríes, Ramón (Prisa's founder; 1934–) 9, **39**
journalism prizes, Grupo Prisa 66–67
Juan Carlos I (King of Spain; 1938–) 4, 10, 51

Kalipedia.com (Prisa's web site) 17
Kiosko y Más (online press platform, Spain) 95

La Factoría (Prisa's subsidiary) 34
La Gazzetta dello Sport (sports newspaper, Italy) 5
La Prensa (newspaper, Mexico) 12, **27**
Lara Hernández, José Manuel (Grupo Planeta's founder; 1914–2003) 4
La Razón (newspaper, Bolivia) 13
La Razón (newspaper, Spain) 53, 78, 104, 106
La Repubblica (newspaper, Italy) 10, 74
La Sexta (private free-to-air television channel, Spain) 82, 104
Latin America: Telefónica in 4; Grupo Prisa in 6, 36, 41, 44n1, 47, 55, 103, 105, 108; Grupo Prisa workers in 57, 62; *El País* newspaper in 8, 65, 93–95; Santillana in 11, 16, 20, 28, 30, **31**, 36, 65–67, 72, 84–86, 88; music market in 13; Prisa radio in 16, 32, 83; Spanish companies in 44, 108
La Vanguardia (newspaper, Spain) 4, 53, 79, 89
La ventana (Cadena SER's radio program) 80
learning systems developed by Santillana 20, 30, 32, 85, 88–89, 98n8, 107
Le Monde (newspaper, France) 10, 13, **28**, **31**, 93, 106, 109n5
Le Monde Libre Société Commandité Simple (publisher, France) 13, 106
Libération (newspaper, France) 61
Liberty Acquisitions Holdings (hedge fund, US) 19, 48, **49**, 56
Llamas, Carlos (former director-presenter of *Hora 25*; 1954–2007) 80
Localia (Prisa's local television) 16, 18, **28**, **29**, 39, 45n9
Los 40/Los 40 Principales (Prisa's musical network) 6, 83, 32, 67, 83, 96, 107; Los 40.com 17; Los 40 Dance 32, 83; LOS40 Music Awards 66
Luca de Tena, Torcuato (Spanish media businessman; 1861–1929) 4

M80 Rádio (musical radio network, Portugal) 17, 34
M80 (Prisa's musical radio network) 32, 83
Macmillan Publishers (publishing company) 85, 86, 88
Marca (sport newspaper, Spain) 5, 104
Marynberg, Zev (former Prisa's investor) 50
Mateu Cromo Artes Gráficas (Santillana's subsidiary) 16
Máxima FM (Prisa's musical radio network) 14, 32, 83
McGraw-Hill (educational publisher) 85, 88
Media Capital (multimedia group, Portugal) 17, 20–21, 24n27, **28**, **29**, 34, 35, **36**, 39, 45n6, 45n10
Media Capital Radio – MCR (radio group, Portugal) 17, **31**, 32, 34

Index 115

media corporations: and bank ownership of 2, 104; global trends for 42; digital challenge and 41
media investments, of Grupo Prisa see diversification
Mediapro (audio-visual group, Spain) 23n20, 40, 54, 68n5
Mediaset (multimedia group, Italy) 3, 4, 39; merger with Mediaset España 5
Mediaset España (multimedia group, Spain) 3, 5, 19, 20, 23n25, **29**, **31**, 41, 44, 45n10; merger with Mediaset 5
Mendo, Carlos (Prisa's founder; 1933–2010) 9, **49**
Meristation (Prisa's magazine) 32, 44n1
Mexico: Gran Vía Musical in 14; Grupo Prisa in **27**; Radiopólis in 16, **28**, **31**, 32, 83; Grupo Norma in 23n23, 44n1; Santillana in 32, 66, 84, 85, 87; *El País* newspaper in 33, 55, 90, 94; Grupo Prisa's revenues from 36; Grupo Prisa's employees in 62; Mexican Roberto Alcántara 41, 96, **58**; *As* sport newspaper in 45n5
Minc, Alain (businessman, France) 56
Mirat, Manuel (current Prisa's CEO) 56, **58**, 88, 98n8, 106
Mondadori (publisher, Italy) 4

National Commission on Markets and Competition – CNMC (Spain) 20, 88
New York Times, The (newspaper, US) 54, 61, 74, 93, 108; article about *El País* in 75–76; nytimes.com 94
Nieto, Alejandro (former Cadena SER's director; 1968–2016) 81
Norma, Grupo Editorial (publisher, Colombia) 16, 23n23, 28, **31**, 44n1, 85; Carvajal Soluciones Educativas 16

Océano, Grupo (publisher, Spain) 85
O Estadão (newspaper, Brazil) 74
Onda Cero (radio network, Spain) 95, 96, 104
Ortega y Gasset, José (Spanish philosopher; 1883–1955) 9; Ortega y Gasset Awards 66
Ortega Spottorno, José (Prisa's founder; 1916–2002) 9, **49**, 102

Oughourlian, Joseph (current Prisa's non-executive vice-chairman; 1972–) **50**, 50, **58**, 107

Panama: Prisa Radio in 16, 32, 80, 83; *El País* newspaper influence in 55
Panama Papers scandal 76, 82
Paramount (cinema US) 38
Partido Popular – PP (political party, Spain) 15, 18, 38, 52, 53–54, 81, 95, 104
Paton, John (Digital Fist Media's CEO, US) 41
pay-TV: Movistar+ and 4; Grupo Prisa and 12, 14–16, 17, 19, 26, **27**, 28, **29**, **31**, 38–41, 43, 102; DTT in Spain and 22n7; Media Capital and 34
Pearson (multinational publisher and education company) 85, 86, 88
Penguin Random House (multinational publisher) **29**, 30, 86, 87
Peña Nieto, Enrique (former Mexican president; 1966–) 55, 85, 86
people.com.cn (online newspaper, China) 94
Pérez González, Francisco (Santillana's founder; 1926–2010) 84
Perú: Grupo Norma in 23n23, 44n1; Prisa radio in **29**; *El País* newspaper in 33, 55, 94; Santillana Educaión in 66; Crisol bookstores in 86
Planeta, Grupo (multimedia holding, Spain) 3, 4, 85, 87, 104; Planeta DeAgostini 87
Plural Entertainment (Media Capital's audio-visual producer) 17, **31**, 34
Podemos (Spanish political party, Spain) 1, 54, 68n6, 75, 77, 78
Podium Podcast (Prisa's subsidiary) 83–84, 107
Polanco, Jesús (former Prisa' president and CEO; 1929–2007) 3, 5, 10–11, 21n5, 47–48, **49**, 51, 54, 102; death of 9, 18, 103; and Santillana 22n8, **27**, 84; family 8, 9, 19, 27, 38, 48, **49**, **50**, 56, 84, 106; pact between Antonio Asensio and 15, 23n19; Jesús de Polanco Chair of Ibero-American Studies 66
Polanco, Manuel (Prisa's director; 1961–) 58

Portugal: Grupo Prisa in 6, **27**, **28**, **29**, 41; Media Capital and 17, **31**, 32, 34; Portugal Telecom or Altice Portugal 21; Santillana in 72, 86, 87
Pradera, Javier (former *El País*' editorial page editor; 1934–2011) 12
Prisa Brand Solutions 34, 44n1
Prisacom 17, 92
Prisa Noticias 32–33, 34, 45n10, 77
Prisa Radio 8, 16, 20, **29**, 32, 45n10, 61, 80, 83–84, 95, 107
Prisa TV 20
Prisa Video 73
PSOE – Spanish Socialist Workers' Party 10; and Grupo Prisa 74; socialist government (PSOE), Grupo Prisa relationship with 15, 43
Público (newspaper, Portugal) 12, **27**
Público (newspaper, Spain) 78, 109n5

Radio Barcelona (radio station, Spain) 18, 66
Radio Caracol (radio network, Colombia) 16, 23n24, **27**, **31**, 80, 83
Rádio Comercial (radio network, Portugal) 17, 34
Radio Continental (radio station, Argentina) 16, **28**, 80
Radio El País (former Prisa's radio network, Spain) 11, 79
Radio Estéreo (radio station, Argentina) 16, **28**
Radiolé (Prisa's musical radio network) 32, 67, 83
Radio Madrid (radio station, Spain) 11, 83
Radio Marca (radio network, Spain) 5
Radio Nacional de España – RNE (public radio network, Spain) 95, 96
Radio Panamá (radio network, Panama) 80
Radiópolis (radio company, Mexico) 16, **28**, **31**
Radio Televisión Española - RTVE (public broadcaster, Spain) 15, 23n26
Rajoy, Mariano (former Spanish president; 1955–) 5, 54, 61, 75, 77, 87, 104
RCS MediaGroup (multimedia group, Italy) 3, 5, 104
Retina (Prisa's magazine) 33, 95

Richmond Publishing (Santillana's subsidiary) 85, 86, 98n1
Rodríguez Zapatero, José Luis (former Spanish president; 1960–) 10, 13, 22n7, 53–54, 74, 81
Rolling Stone (Prisa's musical magazine) 32
Roures, Jaume (Spanish media businessman; 1950–) 68n5

Sánchez, Pedro (current Spanish president; 1972–) 54, 77
Santillana 6, 8, 11, 22n8, 30–32, 72, 84–89, 98n1, 103, 105; integration into Prisa 12, **27**, **27**, 48; purchases of 16, **29**, 55; SantillanaEnRed.com 17; DLJ South American Partners and 18, 20, 87; Bertelsmann and 20, 30, 86–87, ; and learning systems 20, 30, 32, 85, 88–89, 98n8, 107; revenues from **36**, 44, 84, 32; in Latin America 16, **29**, 55, 84–86, 87, 103; Fundación Santillana 55, 65–66, 72, 105
Saramago, José (1998 Nobel Prize in Literature; 1922–2010) 87
Savater, Fernando (Spanish philosopher; 1947–) 12, 79
Semprún, Jorge (former Spanish minister of Culture; 1932–2011) 52
SER – Sociedad Española de Radiodifusión see Cadena SER shareholders of Grupo Prisa 5, 8, 9, 10, 12, 19, 21n3, 21n5, 47–50, **49**, **50**, 76
SModa (Prisa's magazine) 33, 95
Smooth FM (radio network, Portugal) 17, 34
Sogecable (Prisa's audio-visual subsidiary) 14–16, 17, 18, 23n19, 26, 35, 37, 43, 48, 56; contribution to Prisa's debt 16, 17, 37, 38–40, 41, 103, 106; revenues from **36**; agreements with US television stations 38; and Telefónica 39
Solchaga, Carlos (former Spanish minister of Industry; 1944–) 52
Sony Pictures (cinema, US) 38
Soto Ivars, Juan (Spanish writer; 1985–) 76–77

Index 117

Suárez, Adolfo (former Spanish president; 1932–2014) 52
symbolic power 71

Tejero, Antonio (protagonist of the attempted 23-F coup d'état; 1932–) 10, 11, 73; the Tejerazo 10, 72
telecommunication market, liberalization of 4, 15
Telefónica (telecommunications, Spain) 3, 4, 15–16, 52, 56, 66, 103, 105, 107; and Sogecable ownership 16, 39; Movistar+ 4; sale of Digital+ to 19, 20, 23n25, 29, 41, 76; and Vía Digital 23n21, 38; ownership of Grupo Prisa **50**
telegraph.co.uk (online newspaper, UK) **94**
Telemadrid (public regional free-to-air TV, Spain) 81
Televisa (multimedia group, Mexico) 15, 16, **31**, 44
television broadcasting sector, market liberalization of 2, 14, 22n3, 23n19, 37
Televisión Española – TVE (public broadcaster, Spain) 14, 23n19, 51, 81
Times, The (newspaper, UK) 9
Time Warner (multimedia company, US) 38
Tinta Libre (magazine, Spain) 109n5
Toluca, Grupo (holding, Mexico) 41, **58**
transition process in Spain 3, 5, 10, 26, 50–51, 52
Trust and Artisan Partners (bank, US) 48
TVI – Televisão Independente (television company, Portugal) 17, **31**, 34
Twitter (US) 95

Unión Radio (currently Prisa Radio) 13, 16–17, 18, 23n16, **29**, 98n4
United Nations Global Compact 63–64, 68n10
Universal Pictures (cinema, US) 38
Universal Music Group – UMG 56; Grupo Prisa and 14, **28**
university education and Santillana 65–66
UN Sustainable Development Goals – SDGs 68n10; Grupo Prisa and 65

US Hispanic market and Grupo Prisa 13, 19, **31**, 38, 41, 44n1, 45n5

Valcárcel, Darío (Prisa's founder) 9, **49**
Vargas Llosa, Mario (2000 Nobel Prize in Literature; 1936–) 87, 98n7; Mario Vargas Llosa Chair 66
Vía Digital (pay-tv company, Spain) 15–16, 23n21, 38; football wars and 15, 38; merger with CSD 14, 16, **28**
Victoria Capital Partners (former DLJ South American Partners) 30
Villalonga, Juan (former Telefónica's CEO; 1953–) 15
Vivendi Group (multimedia holding, France) 15, 56
V-me Media (Spanish-language broadcast television network, US) 13, 19, **31**, 38, 44n1
Vocento, Grupo (multimedia holding, Spain) 3, 4, 104
Vodafone FM (radio network, Portugal) 17, 34

Wall Street Journal, The (newspaper, US) 93
Washington Post, The (newspaper, US) 93
washingtonpost.com (online newspaper, US) **94**
Washington Post Company (publisher, US) 93, 108
workers of Grupo Prisa 57–63, *60*, 67, 72, 73, 104, 105, 108
W Radio (Prisa's radio network, Colombia) 6

xinhuanet.com (information website, China) **94**

Ya (newspaper, Spain) 89
YouTube (US) 95

Zedillo, Ernesto (former Mexican president; 1951–) 55, 56
Zeta, Grupo (Spain) 3, 23n19

For Product Safety Concerns and Information please contact our EU representative GPSR@taylorandfrancis.com
Taylor & Francis Verlag GmbH, Kaufingerstraße 24, 80331 München, Germany

www.ingramcontent.com/pod-product-compliance
Lightning Source LLC
Chambersburg PA
CBHW051754230426
43670CB00012B/2286